7-Day Country Quilts

Written & Illustrated by
Fran Roen

Sterling Publishing Co., Inc.   New York

I'd like to thank my very best friend, Jah, who has always been there for me; and my wonderful husband, Ron, who is so supportive; and I cannot forget my children—Cressenda, Carry, Caleb, Char, Clint, and Charlie—who, even when busy, take time to look at my quilts and tell me how they feel about them.

The Ribbon Quilt, Indian Homeland, Triple around the World, Mother's Quilt, Shadowed Windows, and Quick Fan are original quilt designs or variations on traditional quilt designs by the author.

Photography by Billy Robin McFarland

Edited by Jeanette Green

Library of Congress Cataloging-in-Publication Data
Roen, Fran.
　7-day country quilts / by Fran Roen.
　　　p.　　cm.
　Includes index.
　ISBN 0-8069-8685-9
　1. Patchwork—Patterns.　2. Machine quilting—Patterns.
I. Title.　II. Title: Seven day country quilts.
TT835.R624　1992
746.9'7—dc20　　　　　　　　　　　　　92-17516
　　　　　　　　　　　　　　　　　　　　　　　　CIP

2　4　6　8　10　9　7　5　3

Published in 1992 by Sterling Publishing Company, Inc.
387 Park Avenue South, New York, N.Y. 10016
© 1992 by Fran Roen
Distributed in Canada by Sterling Publishing
% Canadian Manda Group, P.O. Box 920, Station U
Toronto, Ontario, Canada M8Z 5P9
Distributed in Great Britain and Europe by Cassell PLC
Villiers House, 41/47 Strand, London WC2N 5JE, England
Distributed in Australia by Capricorn Link Ltd.
P.O. Box 665, Lane Cove, NSW 2066
Manufactured in the United States of America

Sterling ISBN 0-8069-8685-9

Contents

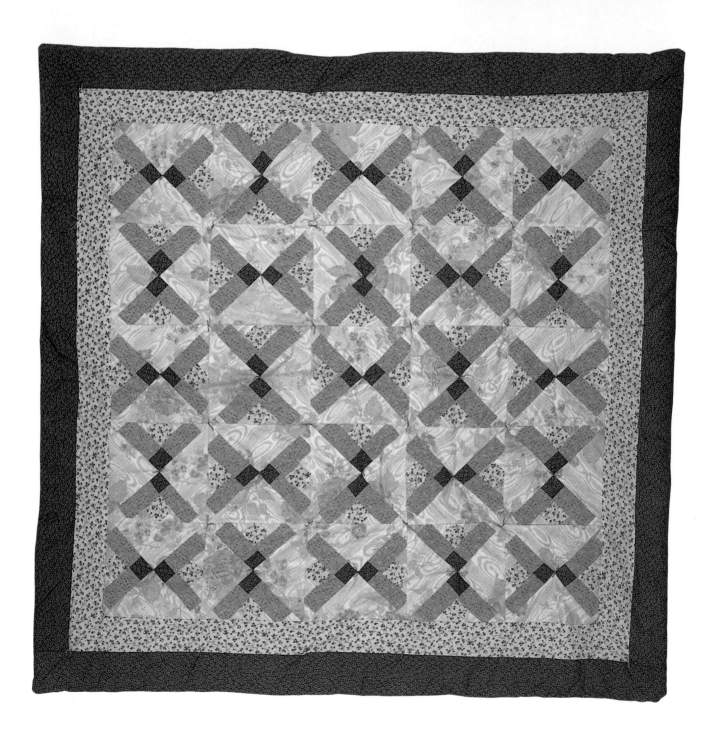

Double Fower Garden, see p. 50.

Introduction

I can still remember my mother's box of quilt pieces—so many different colors and sizes! As a child, I spent a great deal of time looking at them, picking out my favorite prints and colors.

However, now I understand that quilts are more than simply fabric and thread. They are lives and memories, and embody likes and dislikes. They act as bridges from friend to friend, mother to daughter, and generation to generation.

The oldest known pieced work, dated around 930 B.C.E., is in a museum in Cairo. The art of quilting and piecing continued to develop, and in the first century C.E., a Jewish historian, Flavius Josephus, described a beautiful quilted tapestry that hung in the temple Herod built.

Quilting and piecing eventually grew into an art form that every proper lady was expected to master. Even our foremothers carried three most treasured belongings as they crossed the American continent in covered wagons—garden seeds, a Bible, and favorite quilt patterns. (I can easily understand this, since all three things brought comfort and beauty to their often difficult lives.)

Today, technology is king, but the love of traditional quilting and pieced work continues to grow. Although we don't have the time our ancestors did, these speed quilts contain the same romance, accuracy, and quality of the quilts of long ago.

It is my hope that in our constantly changing world, making even one of these quilts will bring you pleasure and satisfaction—especially knowing that you now belong to a long line of quilt makers.

Materials

BACKING

The backing is the bottom or under side of your quilt—usually made of 6 to 7 yards of *100 percent cotton muslin*. Some people like to use a sheet for the back. If you decide to do this, remove all seams and wash the sheet before using it. Always buy the sheet one size larger than the quilt you plan to make.

BATTING

This is the filling that goes between your pieced top and the backing. There are generally two types of batting—cotton and polyester. *Cotton,* the traditional batting, is very nice to work with but not readily available. *Polyester* is equally nice to work with, readily available, and comes in many different styles. There are bonded and unbonded battings and a wide range of lofts—from low to ultra-high. Other types of batting, like fleece, are also available, but for the projects in this book, cotton or polyester battings are the best and most often used.

Have you ever taken your polyester batting out of its plastic bag, then tried to get it back in? It's hard to do, isn't it? That's because, as soon as you take it out of the bag, the batting begins to fill with air—this is called *breathing*. When you open the bag, you'll notice that there may appear to be both thin and clumpy areas. What you need to do is lay the batting out open on a table overnight to allow the batting to breathe. If you don't have the space or time, put the batting in the dryer on the delicate cycle for a few minutes.

COLORS

I like to choose a large-print piece that I really like and build from it. Then I pick out colors from the large print to use in the rest of the quilt. Even if I don't use the large print in the quilt, I know that the colors go together. But it's wise to be careful when using large prints in quilts, since more than one large print may make the quilt appear too busy. Large prints work well in large areas.

Sometimes I use a color wheel that I picked up at an art supply store. But, no matter how you choose your colors, always play the light colors against the dark. For example, if you want the points of a star to show up, you may choose dark points with a light background. Medium colors against medium colors will always blend in and not stand out, even if you use a medium green with a medium yellow. Light against dark or dark against light colors always create a striking quilt.

FABRIC

I prefer to use 100 percent cotton when I'm making a quilt; however, you can use almost any type of fabric for quilting as long as all your choices have the same weight and fabric content.

All fabrics should be prewashed. Check to make sure all your fabric is *color-fast*. If you find you have a bleeder, fill your washing machine to its lowest level with cold water and add a mixture of 1¼ cups of white vinegar and ½ cup of salt (this mixture will set colors nine out of ten times). I allow the fabric to soak for at least four hours, but overnight, when possible, is better. If the fabric still bleeds after this, then label your finished quilt "dry clean only." I prefer to simply choose a different fabric; I want washable quilts.

IRON

Pressing is a must. When pressed, your blocks will be kept flat, without puckers or unwanted folds. It also helps to keep the blocks square. Remember, there is a difference between pressing and ironing. *Pressing* is, just as the word implies, pressing the weight of the iron down on your fabric to achieve an even heat flow. *Ironing* is done with a back-and-forth movement of the iron. With small pieces of fabric used in quilting, ironing may cause them to roll.

NEEDLES

Always keep a good supply of needles on hand. If your sewing machine needle is bent or rough, replace it. Don't wait until it breaks. Generally, I use sewing machine needle sizes 12 and 14. For hand quilting, I use "betweens," needles sized 7–12. For tying your quilt, you will need a large-eyed needle to use with a good quality yarn or embroidery floss.

PRESSING SURFACE

Use an *ironing board* or an *ironing pad*. To make your own ironing pad: Buy an ironing board cover, and measure about 2 feet up from the bottom of the cover, and cut it across. Remove all elastic and square it off. Cut a piece of batting and backing the same size, and sew them together. Now you can press anywhere on the pad without worrying about damaging the surface, such as your kitchen table, that's beneath the pad.

QUILTING PINS

Extra-long quilting pins are the most practical type to use for these projects. Also have a number of *large safety pins* on hand if you plan to hand or machine quilt your project. It will take about 20 to 24 dozen pins to piece together a king-size quilt.

ROTARY CUTTER AND MAT

After the sewing machine, these tools are the most important aids to speedy quilting. *Rotary cutters* are generally sold in two sizes—small and large. There are many sizes of *mats*. Without a mat or cutting board under your fabric, your work surface will become badly scored and your blade will quickly dull.

Jacob's Ladder, see p. 25.

Ribbon Quilt, see p. 47.

RULER

Most patterns in the book require 2½-inch strips, so I went to my local hardware store and had them cut a piece of *Plexiglas* that measures 2½ inches by 27 inches. (I made sure that the piece measured 2½ inches across, down its full length before I left the store.) The best thing to use for quilt making is an *acrylic quilter's ruler*, but these can be expensive. Plexiglas is a very affordable alternative—my piece cost less than two dollars.

SEAM RIPPER

We are all imperfect; this tool allows us to get rid of our mistakes quickly and cleanly. Mine is always nearby.

SCISSORS

It's a good idea to keep a pair of sharp scissors next to your sewing machine. That way, you can cut off small threads right away instead of having to go back and cut them later.

SEWING MACHINE

Any well-running sewing machine will do. If you also have a surger, I would suggest using it, but you can get along just fine without one. Make sure that your sewing machine is well-oiled, the thread tension is on the correct setting, and everything is running smoothly. Nothing seems to stop a project as fast as a poorly operating machine. Unfortunately, most of those stopped projects never seem to get finished.

THREAD

Cotton thread is best, but it is often hard to come by. *Cotton-covered polyester thread* is much more readily available and works equally well. Whatever you choose, remember that you want your quilt to last; so select the best quality of thread that you can afford.

Speed Techniques

ROTARY CUTTER

Lay your cutting mat or board on your work surface. Then lay down your first piece of fabric so that the grain is vertical to you. (Cut all strips with the grain, or from selvage to selvage.) Now lay down the rest of your fabrics, one on top of the other, with all grains aligned. Make sure all fabric is smooth. The rotary cutter can cut through as much as six layers of fabric at one time. Remember that the more fabric you cut at one time, the greater the pressure you'll need to apply to the cutter. (A helpful hint: the more vertical the rotary cutter, the less pressure you'll need.) If you are right-handed, place all your fabric to the right. Then start cutting at the far left, and work towards the right. If you are left-handed, do the opposite.

Before cutting your first strip, even off the edges so that they all line up. Then, using your ruler, measure in 2½ inches from the edge, press down firmly on your ruler, and run your rotary cutter along the ruler's edge. If you did not cut through all layers, go back with your scissors and finish. As you become more experienced, you will learn to apply just the right amount of pressure to avoid this problem.

STRIP SEWING

Choose a pair of strips in complementary colors. With right sides together, sew the length of the strips without cutting them loose from the sewing machine. Simply butt in the next set of strips (see 1), and continue with the other pairs until they are all sewn together. This is a real time-saver.

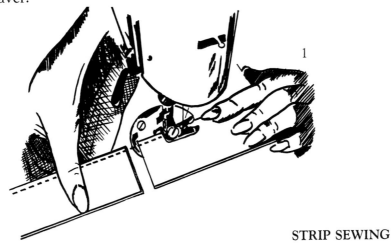

STRIP SEWING

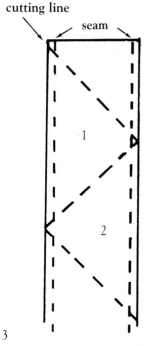

3

SPEEDY TRIANGLE SEWING
Second Method

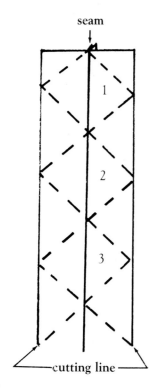

seam

4

SPEEDY TRIANGLE SEWING
Third Method

cutting line

HALF-SQUARE TRIANGLES

First Method To make a half-square triangle (also called a *triangle square*) start by creating a grid on the back of your darkest fabric. If your finished square is supposed to measure 4 inches, then your grid should consist of 5-inch squares. After you've drawn the grid, draw a diagonal line through each of the squares.

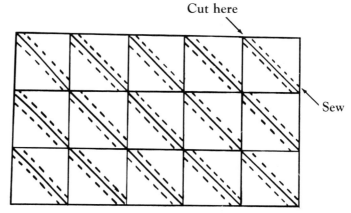

Cut here

Sew

2

SPEEDY TRIANGLE SEWING *First Method*

Next, lay your fabric facedown on a piece of fabric of a complementary light color. Now you are ready to sew the triangles. Line up the fabric on your sewing machine so that the needle is ¼ inch from the first diagonal line, and sew the length of the line. But make sure that you pick up the needle each time you come to the point of another triangle. Do not sew through it. When you have finished the first line, turn your fabric 180 degrees, and sew along the other side of the first diagonal line, making sure to leave a ¼-inch seam allowance. When you have sewn along both sides of all the diagonal lines, then cut along the outlines of the squares and along the diagonal lines. Your triangles are now ready to be pressed and used in your pattern.

Second Method Another way to make a half-square triangle (a *triangle-square*) is to cut two bias strips. If your completed square is to be 4 inches by 4 inches, cut your strips 4½ inches wide, then sew both sides of your strip with a ¼-inch seam allowance. Cut a 4-inch-by-4-inch square, being sure to cut it on the diagonal. Now you have two templates. To cut out your squares, place the base of your template on the seam line and cut. (See 3.)

Third Method A third way to make a half-square triangle (a *triangle square*) also involves cutting two bias strips. Then, sew the length of your strips, with right sides together. Press open with the seam toward the darkest fabric. (The same rule applies for the width of the strips as for the second way to make triangle squares). Cut a 4-inch-by-4-inch square, and lay it out as shown in 4.

DOUBLE HALF-SQUARE TRIANGLES

If the base of your triangle is to be 4 inches and you want it to stand 2½ inches high, cut a 2½-inch-by-45-inch strip. Then cut the strip into 4-inch "rectriangles." Set aside. Since half of 4 inches is 2 inches, cut a 2½-inch-by-45-inch strip of complementary fabrics. Then cut this strip into 2-inch-by-2½-inch "squares." Lay your 4-inch rectriangle faceup on your sewing machine. Place a 2-inch square facedown on the rectriangle, working in the upper right corner, sew at a 45-degree angle to the lower left corner. Repeat this process on the other side, but flip the rectriangle upside down. Cut off the excess and discard. (See 5.)

DIAGONAL QUILTING BY MACHINE

We'll be marking fabric on the bias. If the project is small, marks should be 2 inches apart. If the project is large, marks should be 5 or 6 inches apart. To find the bias of your quilt, lay it on a flat surface so that the grain is vertical to you. Next, fold the right corner over towards the left until the grain of the folded piece is perpendicular to the grain of the fabric underneath. (See 7.) Press very lightly along the fold to create a guideline. Then open the fold, take a ruler, and mark each line with chalk or a pencil at the appropriate distance. (An erasable pen may

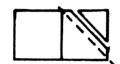

Sew from upper right corner to lower left corner; cut off and discard excess

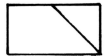

finished seam

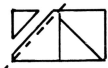

Sew from apex of triangle to base; cut off and discard excess

5

DOUBLE HALF-SQUARE TRIANGLE

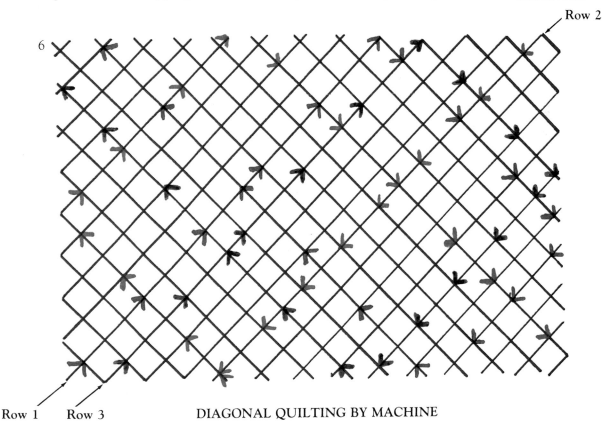

DIAGONAL QUILTING BY MACHINE

Row 2

Row 1   Row 3

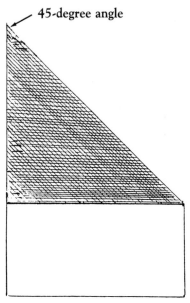

45-degree angle

7   FINDING THE BIAS

leave a line that we cannot see, but eventually that "erased" line may become yellow. I learned this the hard way!)

When you have marked the entire quilt, turn it over, and mark the other side. You should end up with a diamond pattern on both sides. Finally, pin all three layers of fabric together, checking to see that they are secure.

Begin sewing at the upper-left corner and move towards the lower-right corner. Since this is a spiralling technique, start with the largest part of your quilt to the left of the sewing machine. When you have finished your first line, leave the needle in the fabric, raise the pressure foot, and turn the quilt 90 degrees. Move the quilt over so that the needle rests on the second line, lower the presser foot, and sew the length of the line. Repeat this until you have finished the entire top side of your quilt. Then flip it over, and sew the bottom side the same way. When you have finished the bottom, turn the quilt over again and sew the lines that run perpendicular to the ones that you sewed before. Repeat on the bottom until the entire quilt is finished. (See 6.)

MACHINE TYING

Mark your quilt top with a chalk pencil. If you are using cotton batting, mark every 2 to 3 inches. If you are using polyester batting, mark every 5 to 6 inches. Always begin marking in the center of your quilt, and work on a flat surface. Pin around your marks, which are called *tie points.*

When you have finished marking and pinning your quilt, roll the sides of the quilt in toward the middle. This will make it easier to maneuver the quilt. Be sure to lower your machine's feed dogs, and use your regular zigzag stitch. Start sewing at the center of your quilt, and work out toward the edges. Pull both ends of a piece of yarn through the first tie point, and make a knot or bow. Then, lower the presser foot and zigzag over the center of the tie. This is called *bar tacking.* Move to your next tie point, and make another yarn knot or bow and bar tack. When you are finished, clip the loose threads, and remove all pins.

ADDING BORDERS

In this book, all quilt patterns have Amish borders, and most patterns require three borders. To adjust the size of your quilt, you may wish to add or subtract borders.

Here is an example of what the pattern may require and how to handle it:

eight strips 3 inches by 45 inches   *First Border*
eight strips 4 inches by 45 inches   *Second Border*
eight strips 5 inches by 45 inches   *Third Border*

For the first border, pair off your strips, and sew them together on their short ends. Then, sew the first border to the sides and then on top. And, finally, sew the border on the bottom of your quilt. Attach the second border the same way all the way around. And attach the third border the same way.

HANGING YOUR QUILT

To make a casing for your quilt, cut a piece of cotton 6 inches times the finished width of your quilt minus 2 inches. (I put two casings on my quilts—one on the top and one on the bottom. See Helpful Hints to see why.) Hem both short ends. Center the casing on the back of your quilt, and slip-stitch it in place.

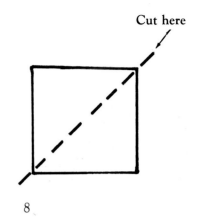

8

BACKING THE QUILT

I have three favorite ways of backing my quilts. The first is *bias binding*. For this method, use a fabric that complements the quilt top.

To make your own bias seam strip, lay the fabric on a flat surface, find the 45-degree bias line. (See 6.) Trim off the bottom, and cut on the diagonal. (See 8.) Sew it back together as shown in 9. Iron flat. (See 10 for cutting.) Your bias strip should be six times wider than you want the finished binding. (For example, if you want a 1-inch binding around your quilt, cut a 6-inch bias strip.) Fold it in half and iron flat. Pin the binding around your quilt with the raw edge towards the outside of your quilt. If your binding is to be 1 inch, then your seam allowance must be 1 inch. Sew on the binding all the way around, cut the quilt free from the machine. Bring the binding around to the other side and stitch it into place.

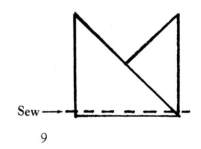

9

A second method involves *laying the backing wrong side up*. Then lay the batting on top of it and the quilt on top of that. Trim the batting to fit the quilt, and make the backing 2 inches larger around the quilt's perimeter. Fold the backing over both the batting and the quilt top, and form a ¼ inch hem from the backing material. Sew all the way around.

The third method is the *pillow-case method*. This is fast and easy. To begin, lay your batting down on the floor, then your backing faceup, and, finally, your quilt facedown on top of the backing. Pin and sew the edges of all three layers, with your machine set for 10 to 12 stitches per inch. Sew all the way around except for a 3-foot opening on one side. Cut your quilt free from the machine, and trim the batting close to the stitching. Roll the corners and sides tightly towards the opening, and pull the whole quilt through the hole. Flatten your quilt, and slip-stitch the opening.

Fabric needed for backing is generally 6 to 7 yards.

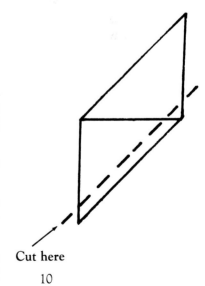

10

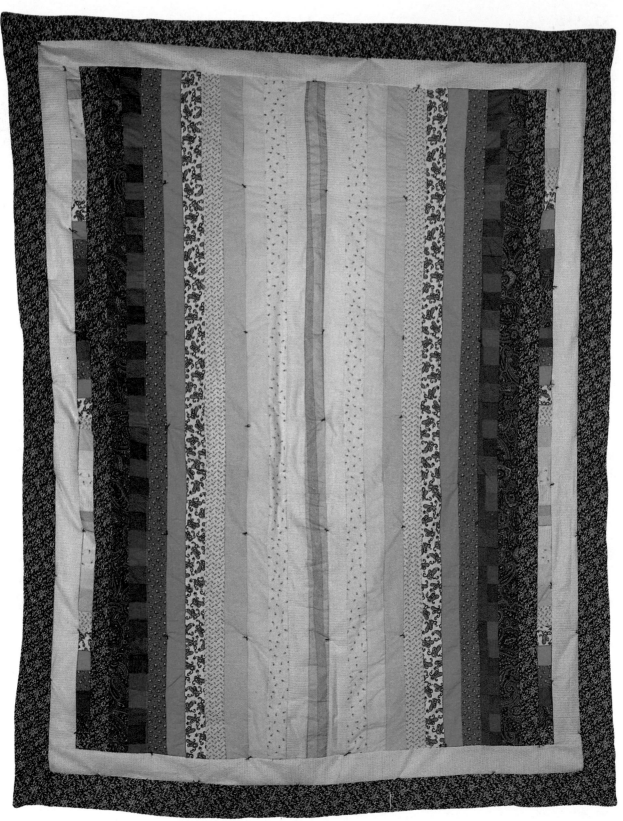

Amish Bar Quilt (70 × 86 inches)

1   Amish Bar Quilt

The Amish Bar Quilt is the easiest quilt to make in this book. It can be a very lovely quilt, perhaps because of its simplicity and balance. When it comes to quilting, we owe a lot to the Amish. They have helped preserve many patterns that might otherwise have been lost.

YARDAGE

Eleven different fabrics (5½ yards total) Fabrics A to K	½ yard each
Center strip (Fabric L)	¼ yard
First border	1 yard
Second border	1¼ yards

CUTTING

From each fabric A to K	four strips 3 × 45 inches
Center strip	two strips 3 × 45 inches
First border	eight strips 4 × 45 inches
Second border	nine strips 5 × 45 inches

SEWING DIRECTIONS

Sew the short ends of fabric A together. So you no longer have four 3-inch-by-45-inch strips but you have two 3-inch-by-90-inch strips. Do this with fabrics A to L.

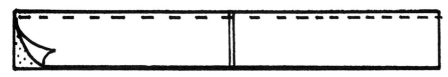

1–1

Sew the strips together: Begin with the center strips, and attach fabric A by sewing the length of the two pieces with right sides together.

Sew the rest of the strips together as shown in 1–1 and 1–2. After the strips are sewn, press well. (I press when I'm half done as well as after I've completed sewing the strips. This makes the final pressing easier.)

Paddle Wheel, see p. 22.

Amish Bar Quilt

Even off the top of your sewn strips (see 1–3) by cutting off excess material to form the body of your quilt. Measure down 72 inches from the top. Now, cut off the bottom so that the body of the quilt will be 72 inches long. Be sure that your quilt body measures an even 72 inches all the way across. This may take time, but it's worth it.

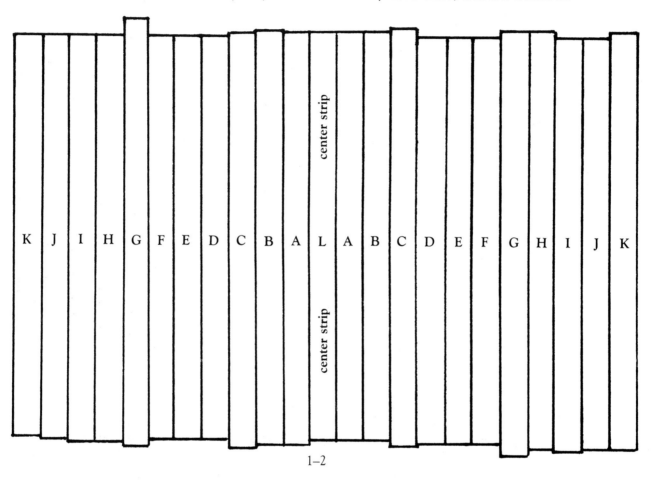

1–2

Sew the short ends of the borders, and attach them according to directions in the Speed Techniques section of this book (p. 14).

Finish the quilt as you like. But there's no need to stop with this one, since many varieties of easy quilts await you.

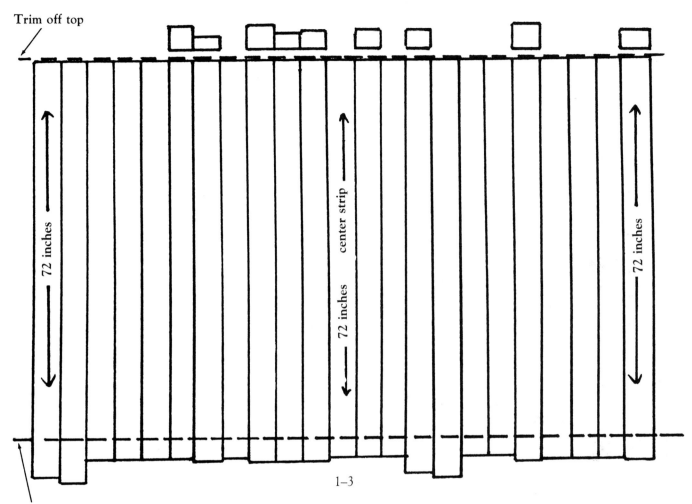

Trim off top

72 inches

center strip

72 inches

72 inches

1–3

Trim off excess from bottom

21

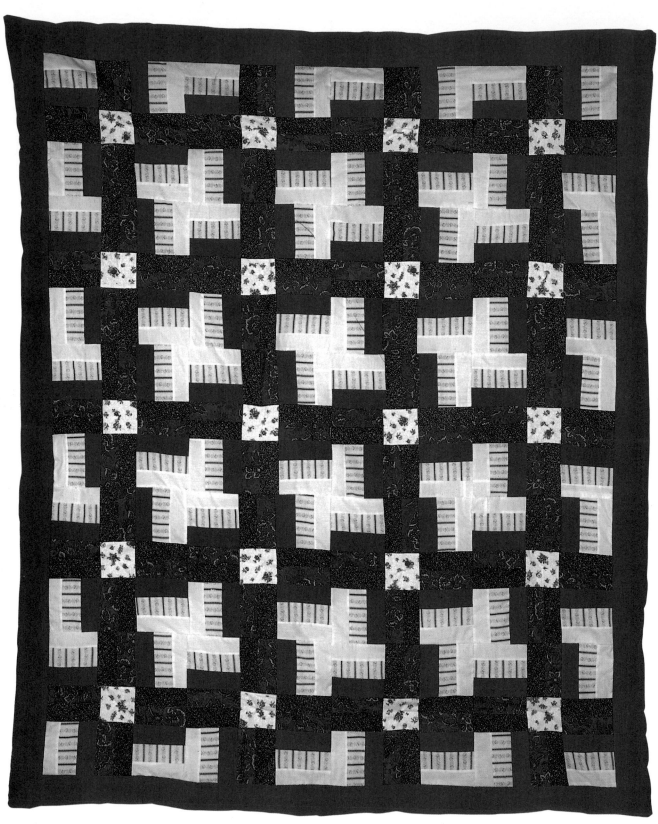

Paddle Wheel (70 × 84 inches)

2 Paddle Wheel

The Paddle Wheel is a very easy quilt, and it can produce many different looks, depending on the colors you choose and the way you arrange them. Quilts help document history; this pattern became popular around the mid-1880s. That was when steamships with paddle wheels floated up and down the Ohio, Mississippi, St. Lawrence, and other rivers.

YARDAGE

Fabrics A to E	1¼ yards each
Fabric F	½ yard
First border	1½ yards

CUTTING

Fabrics A to E	fourteen strips 2½ × 45 inches
Fabric F	three strips 4½ × 45 inches
First border	eight strips 5 × 45 inches

SEWING DIRECTIONS

1. Read how to sew strips under Speed Techniques (p. 11), then sew seven sheets of strips in this order: A B C D E.
   Then press seams flat and measure down 6½ inches, and cut. Do this forty times. Set aside.

2. Sew seven sheets of strips in this order: A B C. Press flat, measure down 6½ inches and cut. Do this forty times. Set aside.

3. Sew seven sheets of strips in this order: D E. Press flat, measure down 6½ inches, and cut. Do this forty times. Set aside.

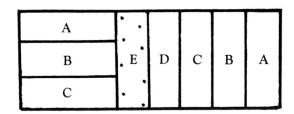

2–1

4. Lay one piece from step 1 faceup on the sewing machine with the strips vertical and fabric E to the right. Place a piece from step 2 facedown with fabric C to the top. Sew down the side. Repeat forty times in all. Your finish piece, which is the top and bottom to your square, should look like 2–1. Press and set aside.

5. Lay a fabric F strip faceup on your machine, and place facedown a 6½-inch piece from step 3 with fabric E to the top of the strip. Sew down the short end. Butt in another piece until you have sewn twenty pieces to a fabric F strip. Cut apart where directed in 2–2.

6. Place faceup a piece from step 5 with the center square to the right. Lay facedown a piece from step 3 with fabric E to the top. Do this twenty times. Your center strip should look like 2–3.

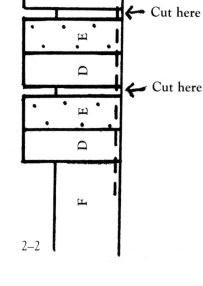

← Cut here

← Cut here

2–2

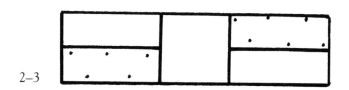

2–3

7. Sew a piece from step 6, sandwiched in between two pieces from step 4. Your finished square should look like 2–4.

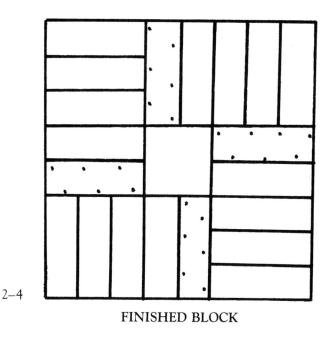

2–4

FINISHED BLOCK

8. Your quilt top will have five rolls, and each roll will have four blocks. Add borders and finish as you like.

3 Jacob's Ladder

When it is created in soft colors, this can be a lovely baby's quilt. Men seem to enjoy it in bold colors.

Be careful about how you lay out the triangle-squares to form the ladder. This quilt, which borrows its name from the Bible, seems to have come to America in the mid- to late 1600s. This suggests that the Jacob's Ladder design was created at a much earlier date somewhere in Europe.

YARDAGE

Fabric A	1¼ yards
White fabric	2½ yards
Fabric B	1¼ yards
First border	¾ yard
Second border	1 yard
Third border	1½ yards

CUTTING

White (remaining white will be used for triangles)	fifteen strips 2½ × 45 inches
Fabric B	fifteen strips 2½ × 45 inches
First border	eight strips 3 × 45 inches
Second border	eight strips 4 × 45 inches
Third border	eight strips 5 × 45 inches

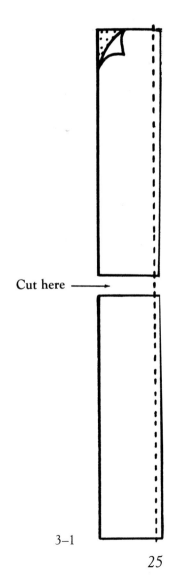

Cut here ⟶

3–1

SEWING DIRECTIONS

1. Place the uncut white fabric faceup on your work surface. Place fabric A facedown on the white fabric. On the back of fabric A, graph a 5-inch-square grid, following directions on how to sew right triangles. Sew and cut as directed. Press open with seams toward the darkest fabric. (You'll need 80 "triangle-squares.") Divide into two equal piles, and set aside.

2. Place your white strips faceup on your sewing machine with fabric B strip facedown. Sew the length of the strips. Follow directions for chain stitching. Sew all your strips together in pairs. (See 3–1.)

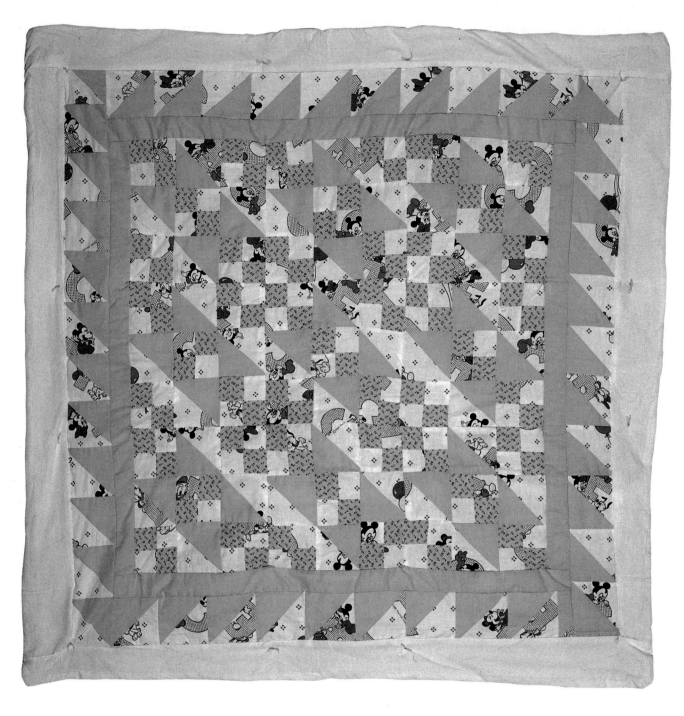

Jacob's Ladder (62 × 62 inches)

3. Measure 2½ inches down your sewn strips, and cut. You'll need to cut your strips into 2½-inch sewn blocks (See 3–2.)

Press open with seams toward the darkest fabric.

4. Sew these sewn blocks together to form a square. (You will need 100 block squares.) (See 3–3.) Press open.

5. Place a block square faceup on your sewing machine with the dark block in the upper right corner. Now take one pile of triangle-squares, and place a triangle-square facedown on your block square with the white triangle in the lower left corner. Sew down the side, and flash feed the same way until all triangle-squares from one pile are attached to a block square. (See 3–4.) Cut the finished blocks free from each other after chain-stitching, and press them open.

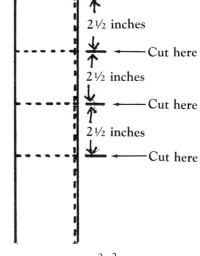

3–2

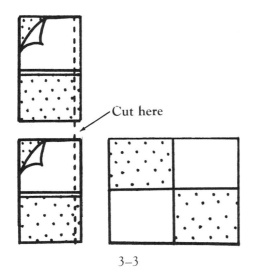

3–3

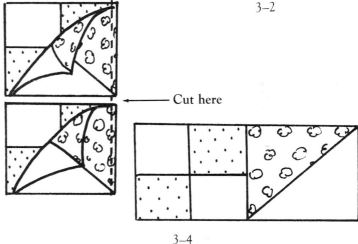

3–4

6. Place your newly sewn block faceup on the machine with the triangle-square to the right. Place a block square facedown with a white square in the upper right corner. (See 3–5.)

Sew a block square to all the newly sewn blocks. Cut them free from each other, press them open, and set them aside. (These will be the top and bottom strips to your block. So, in step 9, when I ask for a top or bottom I mean one of these.)

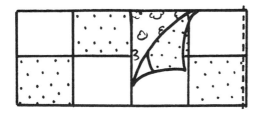

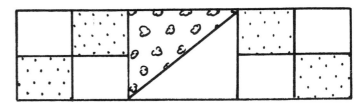

3–5

7. Working with your second pile of triangle-squares, place a triangle-square faceup on your sewing machine with the darkest triangle in the lower right corner. Top with a block square facedown with a white block in the upper right corner. (See 3–6.) Sew down the length. Sew a total of twenty of these combinations. Cut them free from each other, and press them open.

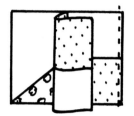
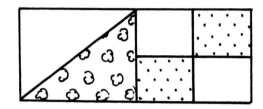

3–6

8. Place your newly sewn combinations faceup on your machine with the block square to the right. Place a triangle-square facedown with the dark triangle in the upper right corner. (See 3–7.) Sew down the length until all sewn combinations have a second triangle-square attached. Cut them free from each other and press seams open. These are your center strips.

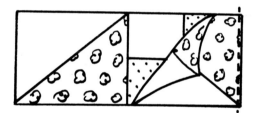
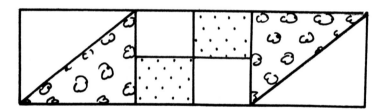

3–7

9. Place a piece from step 6 faceup on your machine with a white block in the right corner and the triangle-square (with the dark triangle in the upper right corner). (See 3–8.) With right side down, place a center strip on top of your top strip. Place it with the triangle-square having the darker triangle in the lower right corner. (See 3–9.)

Sew until all twenty center strips are attached to a top strip. Cut them free from each other, and press seams open.

10. Now place your newly sewn combination faceup on the sewing machine with the center strip towards the right. Place a bottom strip facedown with the block square having the dark block to the right side. Sew all twenty combinations this way. Cut them free from each other, and press seams open. (See 3–10.)

You should have twenty completed blocks.

11. Your quilt top will be made of five rolls of blocks, with each roll made up of four blocks.

See directions on p. 14 for attaching borders. Finish the quilt as you like.

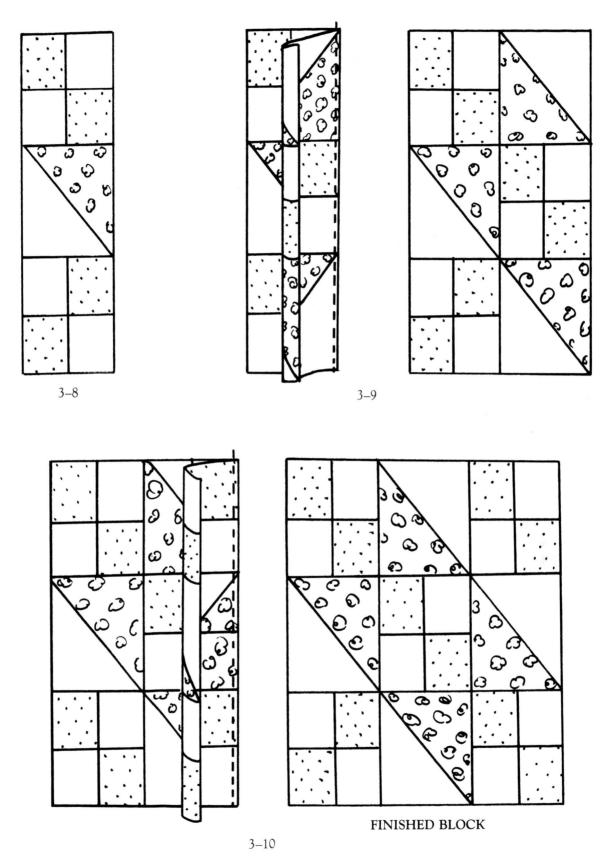

3–8

3–9

3–10

FINISHED BLOCK

Tumbling Blocks (57×71 inches)

4 Tumbling Blocks

This type of quilt was quite popular in the 1800s. It draws on our understanding of perspective and can, with light, medium, and dark color variations, present a wide variety of geometric designs. This quilt, Tumbling Blocks, is for the more advanced or adventurous. That's not because it's any harder than the other quilts in this book, but because it demands more patience. This pattern requires a lot of pivoting.

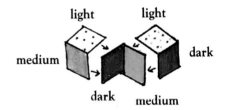

YARDAGE

Light color	1¼ yards
Medium color	1¼ yards
Dark color	1¼ yards
First border	1 yard
Second border	1½ yards
Third border	2 yards

CUTTING

From each of the light, medium, and dark fabrics	fourteen strips 2½ × 45 inches
First border	eight strips 4 × 45 inches
Second border	eight strips 5 × 45 inches
Third border	eight strips 6 × 45 inches

SEWING DIRECTIONS

You have a total of forty-two 2½-by-45-inch strips; sew these in pairs by placing right sides together and sew the length of the strips. Avoid sewing two light, two medium, or two dark colors together. You can chain-stitch the strips in your sewing machine. (See 4–1.)

Cut these strips at a 60-degree angle. If you have a cutting board with a 60-degree angle on it, that's great. You'll want to use it. If not, I've included a worksheet for you. Photocopy the worksheet (See p. 35.) and trace the 60-degree line, as well as the dashed 2½-inch lines, onto heavy cardboard as your cutting board. Place your sewn strips along your 60-degree line. (I cut three sewn strips at a time.) Trim off the top and cut down the strip at the dashed lines for 2½-inch measurements. (See 4–2.) Be as accurate as possible.

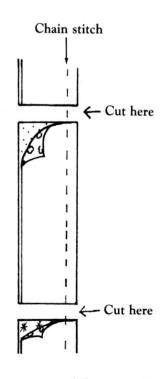

4–1

Since you had twenty-one sewn strips, you should get twelve partial blocks from each strip, which will give you two hundred fifty-two partial blocks.

Press each of these partial blocks open with the seams towards the darkest color.

We'll be sewing 3 partial blocks together to form a set. Your quilt will require 84 sets total.

If you look at 4–3 to 4–5, these directions will be easier to follow.

Place partial block 1 faceup on your sewing machine. Then lay partial block 2 facedown, so that the upper half of block 2 can be sewn to the right upper side of block 1. Allow the top to overlap the seam by ¼ inch. Sew down the length of the block, and stop with your needle in the seam of partial block 2. Pivot partial block 2 around so that its lower left edge is even with the right edge of partial block 1. Make sure the fabric is smooth and then sew. (This can be done with flash feeding. I work six at a time, instead of 84, since it helps me avoid monotony.)

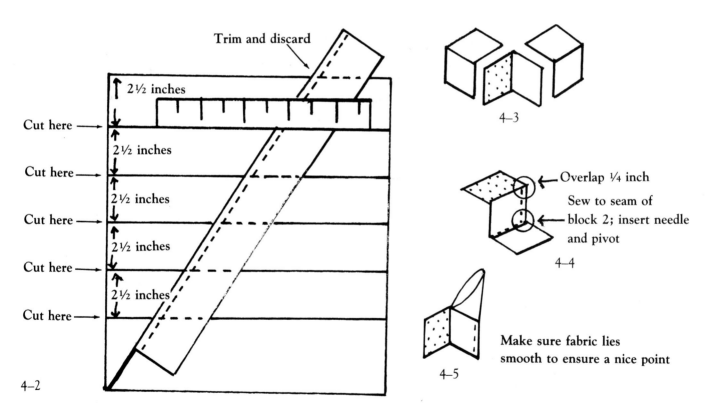

Trim and discard

2½ inches

Cut here →

2½ inches

Cut here →

2½ inches

Cut here →

2½ inches

Cut here →

2½ inches

Cut here →

4–2

4–3

Overlap ¼ inch

Sew to seam of block 2; insert needle and pivot

4–4

Make sure fabric lies smooth to ensure a nice point

4–5

Flip your sewn partial block over, and add your partial block 3 in the same way. When you've finished, you will have a set. Continue until all your partial blocks are sewn into sets for 84 sets in all. It is important to press the sets well before you go on to the next step.

Your quilt top consists of six sets across, forming one roll, fourteen rolls deep.

Tumbling Blocks

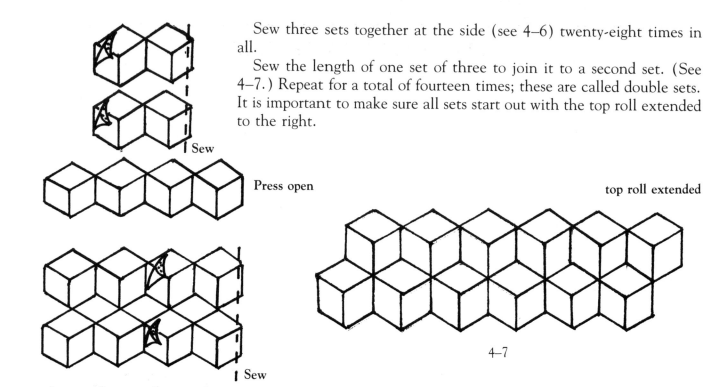

Sew three sets together at the side (see 4–6) twenty-eight times in all.

Sew the length of one set of three to join it to a second set. (See 4–7.) Repeat for a total of fourteen times; these are called double sets. It is important to make sure all sets start out with the top roll extended to the right.

Sew

Press open

top roll extended

4–7

Sew

Press open

4–6

Now sew the short ends of two double rolls together. Repeat seven times to make eight pieces. (See 4–8.)

Sew your long double sets together lengthwise until they complete the six-sets-across, fourteen-rolls-deep top for your quilt.

Even off your sides so that the borders may be added. (See 4–9.)

Reread the section on borders (p. 14) under Speed Techniques, and attach borders as directed. Finish as you wish.

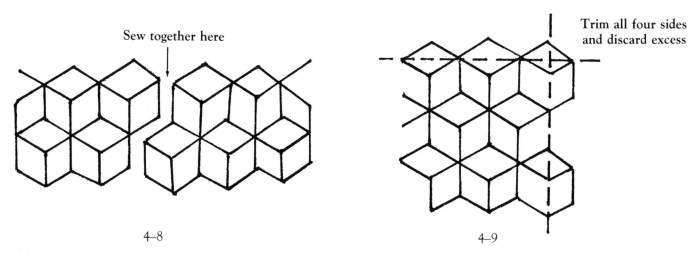

Sew together here

Trim all four sides and discard excess

4–8

4–9

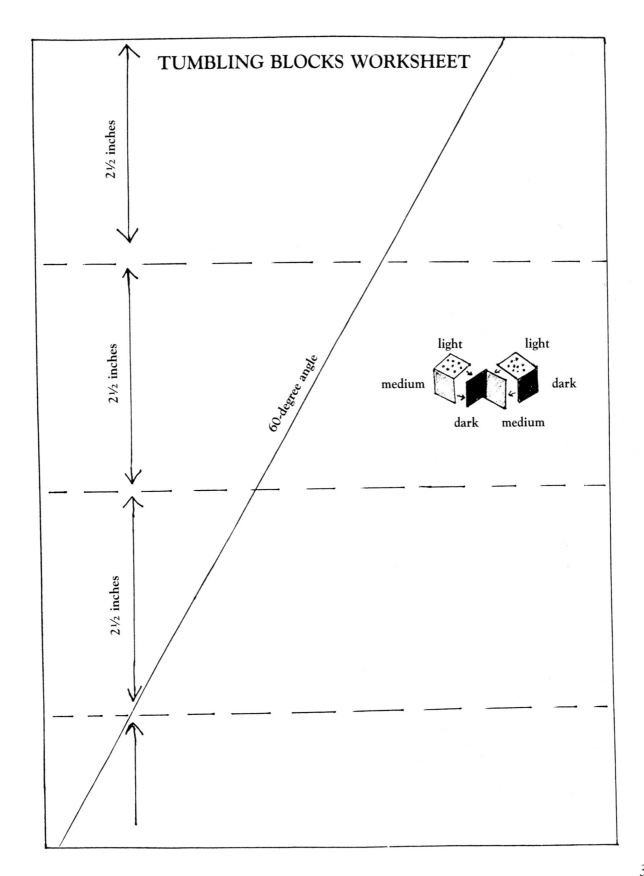

TUMBLING BLOCKS WORKSHEET

2½ inches

2½ inches

2½ inches

60-degree angle

light

light

medium

dark

dark

Triple around the World (74 × 88 inches)

5 Triple around the World

This is truly an easy quilt to make. Both Triple around the World and Tumbling Blocks are examples of all-over quilts. *That means that one small piece is repeated all over the quilt to create the finished design. This quilt was quite popular in the 1800s.*

YARDAGE

Fabrics A to C and E to G	¾ yard each
Fabric D (darkest fabric)	2 yards
First border	1 yard
Second border	1½ yards
Third border	2 yards

CUTTING

Fabrics A to C and E to G	ten strips 4 × 45 inches each
Fabric D	thirty strips 4 × 45 inches
First border	eight strips 3 × 45 inches
Second border	eight strips 4 × 45 inches
Third border	eight strips 5 × 45 inches

| A | B | C | D | D | D | E | F | G | A |

5–1   **Sheet 1**

SEWING DIRECTIONS

Pin a small swatch of fabric to a piece of paper next to its corresponding letter. This will give you a handy reference guide, or worksheet.

Sew your strips into sheets. Referring to both your worksheet and to 5–1, sew the strips together lengthwise in this order:

A B C D D D E F G A

Then press the seams toward the darkest color. Pin a small sheet of paper to this sheet, label it sheet 1, and set aside.

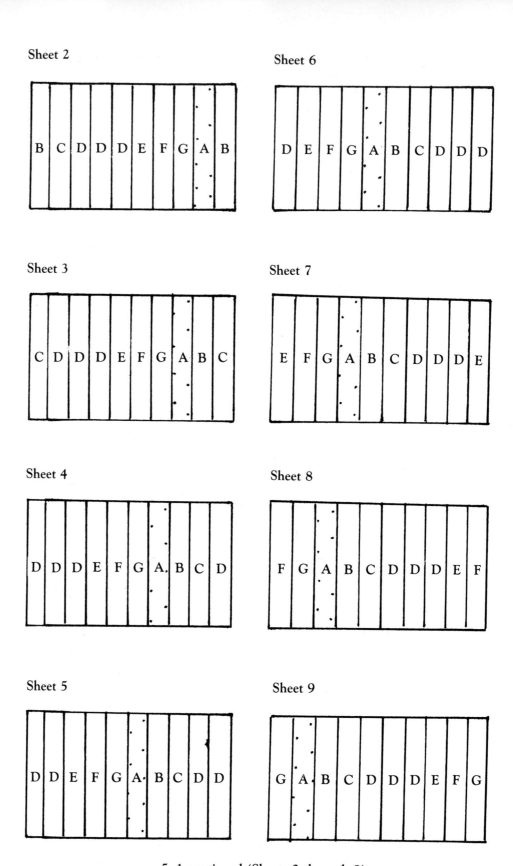

Sheet 2

B C D D D E F G A B

Sheet 6

D E F G A B C D D D

Sheet 3

C D D D E F G A B C

Sheet 7

E F G A B C D D D E

Sheet 4

D D D E F G A B C D

Sheet 8

F G A B C D D D E F

Sheet 5

D D E F G A B C D D

Sheet 9

G A B C D D D E F G

5–1 continued (Sheets 2 through 9)

Next, sew eight more sheets the same way described above, in the following order:

Sheet 2—B C D D D E F G A B
Sheet 3—C D D D E F G A B C
Sheet 4—D D D E F G A B C D
Sheet 5—D D E F G A B C D D
Sheet 6—D E F G A B C D D D
Sheet 7—E F G A B C D D D E
Sheet 8—E G A B C D D D E F
Sheet 9—G A B C D D D E F G

Press each sheet with the seams toward the darkest color and label.

For the next step, first see 5–2. Then measure 4 inches down from the top of your sewn sheet 1. Make sure that the line you just marked is 4 inches all the way across the sheet. Now cut across that line. You should now have a strip of squares. Continue to measure and cut strips until you have four strips of squares from sheet 1. Stack these in a pile and mark them with the sheet 1 label. Now cut the remaining sheets the same way, making sure to label each stack for easy identification.

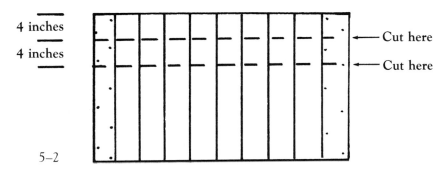

4 inches

4 inches ← Cut here

← Cut here

5–2

Your sheets were cut horizontally, and now sew them vertically. Use your worksheet and 5–3 as a guide. The letters indicated in 5–3 are the

A	G	F	E	D	D	D	C	B	C	D	D	D	E	F	G	A
G	F	E	D	D	D	C	B	A	B	C	D	D	D	E	F	G
F	E	D	D	D	C	B	A	G	A	B	C	D	D	D	E	F

5–3 Sheet 1 Sheet 9 Sheet 8 Sheet 7 Sheet 6 Sheet 5 Sheet 4 Sheet 3 Sheet 2 Sheet 3 Sheet 4 Sheet 5 Sheet 6 Sheet 7 Sheet 8 Sheet 9 Sheet 1

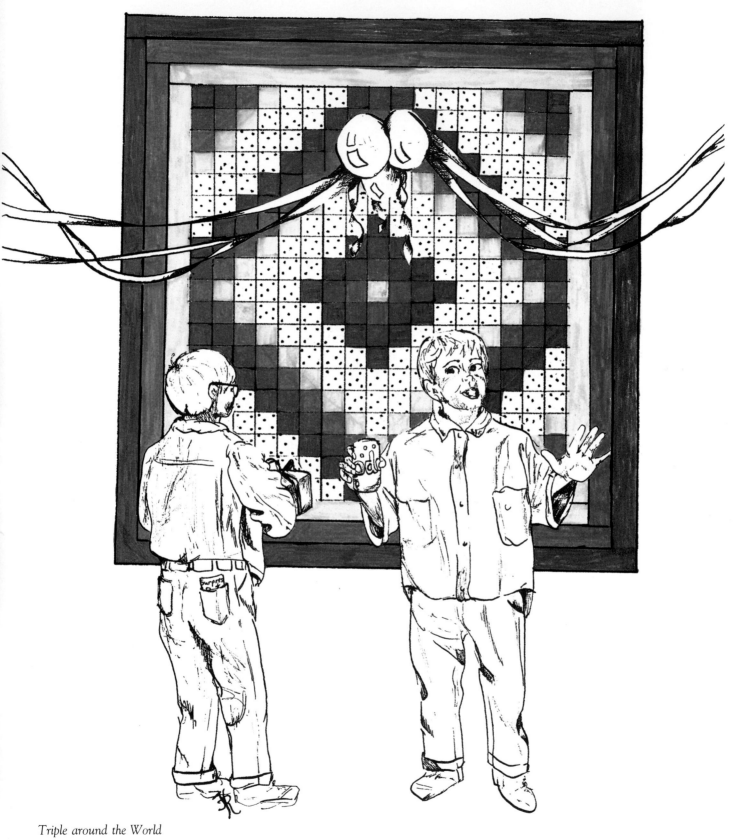

Triple around the World

Mother's Quilt, see p. 43.

last three blocks in each strip. They should provide a visual aid for piecing the quilt. That is why the rest of the blocks are not drawn in. Sew together all the strips shown, and then sew the second set of strips. These blocks will form the upper and lower halves of your quilt.

You should have two strips left over from sheet 2. You will use these to make the center roll. First remove squares A and B from their places, and separate one of the A's from the B. This A will be sewn in the center of your roll.

Sew the strips together so that the squares are in the following order: G F E D D D C B A B C D D D E F G. (See 5–4 for a visual guide.)

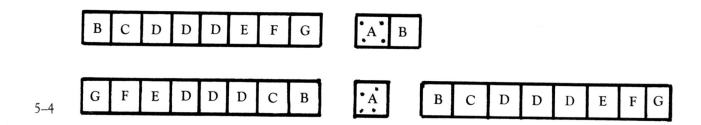

5–4

Sew the center row to the upper half, making sure to match up seams on the squares. Then join the center row and the lower half. Attach the borders (see p. 14), and finish the quilt with the method you prefer.

6 Mother's Quilt

This quilt is more difficult than most, but that's only because it requires combining two different basic quilt patterns described in this book, the Flower Basket (p. 78) and the Multiblock (p. 54). It is a nice example of a framed quilt. Framed quilts made a strong showing between the 1840s and 1890s. They acquired the name framed quilts because they contained a series of borders or frames within the body of the quilt.

This quilt is nice and big; it's for the person who has already made a few quilts in this book. The fabric letters are the same for all three patterns, unless otherwise indicated. This will allow you to follow directions more easily.

YARDAGE

Fabric A	2½ yards
Fabric B	2¼ yards
Fabric C (large flower print)	1½ yards
Fabric D	¾ yard
First border	1 yard
Second border	1½ yards

CUTTING

Fabric A (first diagonal border and second inside border)	eight strips 4 × 45 inches
Fabric A	fourteen strips 2½ × 45 inches
Fabric B	twelve strips 2½ × 45 inches
Fabric B	four strips 8 × 8 inches
Fabric B (second diagonal border)	two strips 4 × 45 inches
Fabric C	six strips 2½ × 45 inches
Fabric C	four strips 8 × 8 inches
Fabric C (third inside border)	four strips 3 × 45 inches
Fabric C (third diagonal border)	two strips 4 × 45 inches
Fabric D (first inside border)	eight strips 2½ × 45 inches

Graph and cut out squares 3 × 3 inches from Fabrics A and B (fourteen across and three down); you'll need eighty triangle-squares.

Mother's Quilt (68 × 78 inches)

SEWING DIRECTIONS

Make eight flower baskets using directions for the Flower Basket quilt. Press the finished blocks and set them aside.

Make sixteen multiblocks using the directions for the Multiblock quilt. Press the finished blocks and set them aside.

Sew four of the flower baskets together as shown in the photo. Attach the first diagonal border, using fabric A, 4-inch strips as shown in 6–1. Trim corners as indicated.

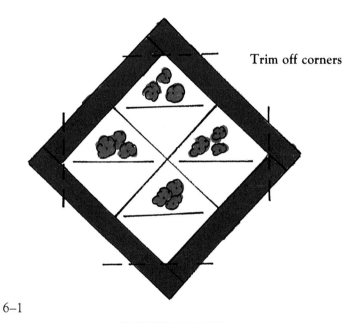

Trim off corners

6–1

FLOWER BLOCK

Attach the 4-inch fabric B diagonal border, and trim it the same as the first diagonal border. Follow up with the last diagonal border out of fabric C, and trim. You should now have a large center square.

Follow directions for attaching borders in the Speed Techniques section, pp. 14–15. Attach the inside borders, starting with 2½-inch fabric A strips and ending with 3-inch fabric C strips. Press and set aside.

Sew your multiblocks into long strips consisting of four squares per strip. (See 6–2.) Attach two flower baskets, one on each end of two strips of blocks as shown in 6–3.

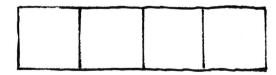

6–2

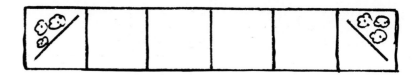

6–3

Attach the short strips to the sides of your large center square. Now attach the longer strips to the top and bottom. Press them flat, and attach the outside borders. (See p. 14.) Finish as you like.

7 Ribbon Quilt

This quilt is fairly easy to make. I stumbled upon this pattern while trying to create a completely different one. I know you will enjoy making it.

YARDAGE

Fabrics A to F	⅔ yard
First border	¾ yard
Second border	1 yard
Third border	1½ yards

CUTTING

From each of fabrics A to F, for forty-two strips	seven strips 2½ × 45 inches
First border	six strips 4 × 45 inches
Second border	eight strips 4 × 45 inches
Third border	eight strips 5 × 45 inches

Cut the remaining sheet of strips into 3-inch widths. Sew the short ends together, and use them as a border.

SEWING DIRECTIONS

Sew your strips lengthwise. Make a sheet of strips, sewing one strip from each of the six different fabrics to form one sheet. Repeat seven times. Press the strips flat.

Measure across your sheet of strips, and whatever that measurement is, measure down that distance and cut. (For example: If your sheet of strips is 12 inches wide, measure down 12 inches, and cut as shown in 7–1.)

You will need eighteen blocks. (The remaining sheet of strips can be used for a pieced second border or used in case you make a wrong cut.)

Put them into two piles, with nine blocks per pile. Cut each pile on the bias in different directions. See 7–2, and label your triangles A, B, C, and D, as shown.

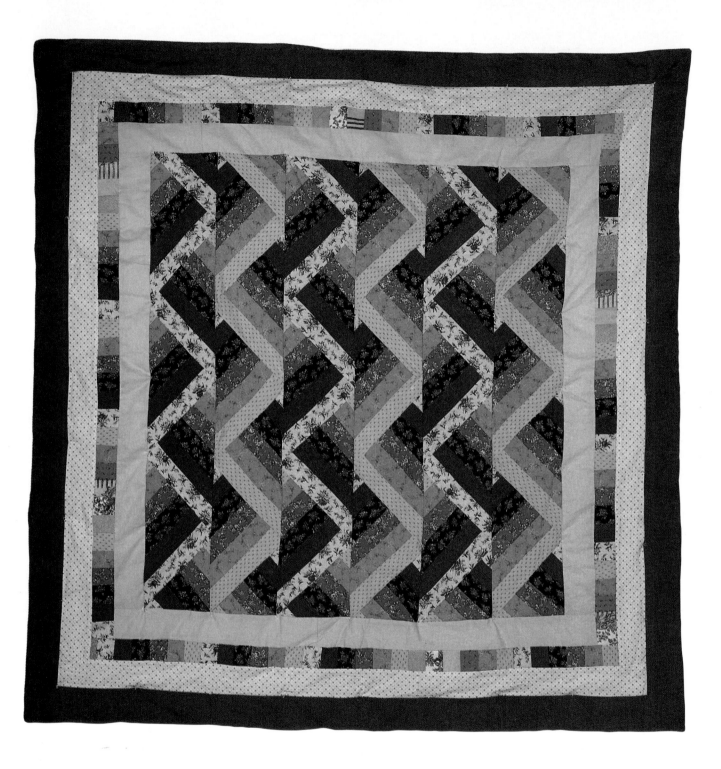

Ribbon Quilt (72 × 76 inches)

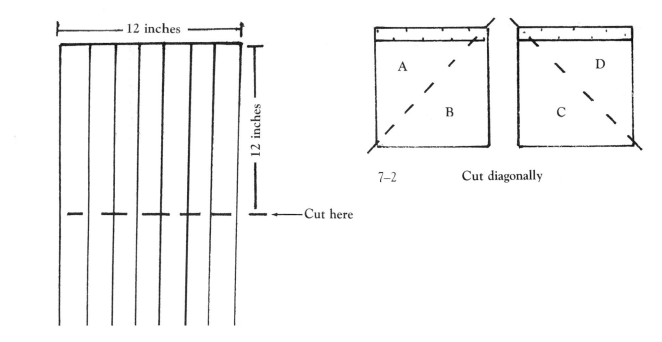

7–1

7–2   Cut diagonally

Find construction for roll 1 in 7–3. Repeat roll 1 three times. Press and set aside.

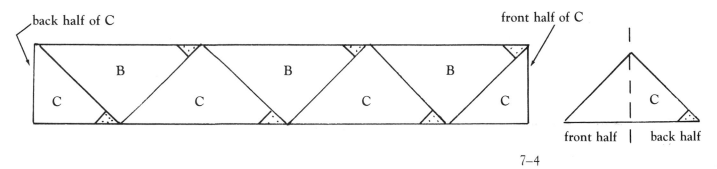

7–3

Find construction for roll 2 in 7–4. Repeat roll 2 three times. Press and set aside.

7–4

Sew your rolls together, alternating rolls 1 and 2 until all rolls are attached to each other.

Add borders according to directions (p. 14).

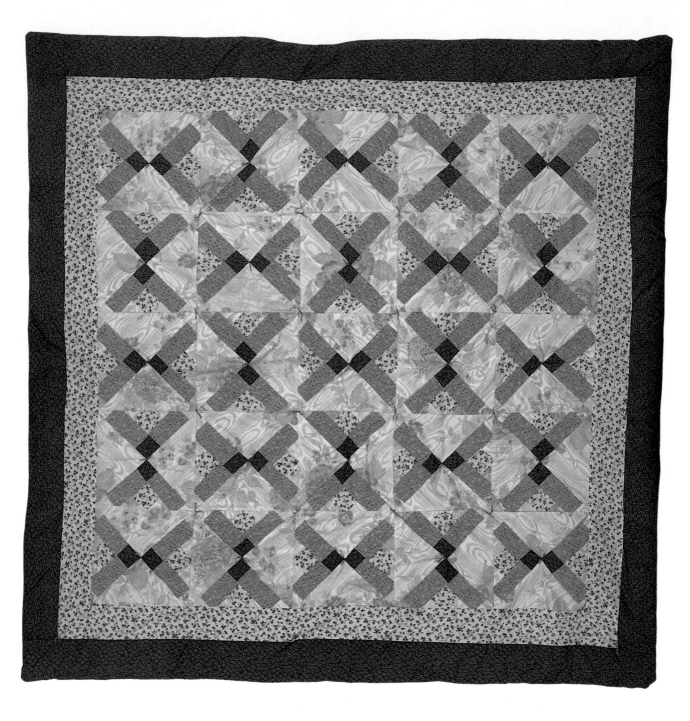

Double Flower Garden (66 × 66 inches)

8 Double Flower Garden

This lovely quilt is one of my favorites, and it is fairly easy to make. In the 1790s it became popular to have unpadded day quilts and top covers for beds. This practice remained popular for almost 35 years.

YARDAGE

Fabric A	1½ yards
Fabric B	1 yard
Fabric C	1 yard
Fabric D	2 yards

CUTTING

Fabric A	three strips 2½ × 45 inches
Fabric B	three strips 4½ × 45 inches
Fabric B	six strips 2½ × 45 inches
Fabric D (then cut on the diagonal)	twenty-five strips 8 × 8 inches
Fabric C (first border)	eight strips 4 × 45 inches
Fabric A (second border)	eight strips 5 × 45 inches

SEWING DIRECTIONS

1. Sew three sheets of strips in this order: Strip A, 4½-inch strip B, strip D. Press flat, measure down 2½ inches and cut for a total of seventeen cuts per sheet, set aside.

2. Again sewing 3 sheets of strips in the following order: 2½-inch strip B, strips C and D, 2½-inch strip B. Press flat, measure down 2½ inches, and cut for a total of seventeen cuts per sheet.

3. Sew your cut pieces from steps 1 and 2 together so that it looks like 8–1. Repeat until all cut pieces are sewn together.

8–1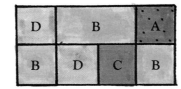

4. Sew your pieces from step 3 together so that fabric D runs diagonally through your square. (See 8–2.) You now have an 8-inch-by-8-inch piece square. Even up the ends if necessary. (You should have twenty-five squares.)

Press and cut on the diagonal through the D squares. (See 8–3.)

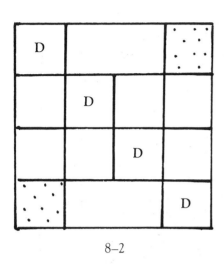

8–2

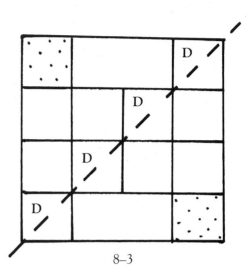

8–3

5. Sew your pieced triangle to a solid triangle as shown in 8–4. Repeat this for a total of fifty times.

6. Sew two pieces from step 5 together so that they look like 8–5. Then, sew your blocks together, five blocks to a roll, five rolls to a quilt.

Add borders as directed (p. 14), then back and finish the quilt as you like.

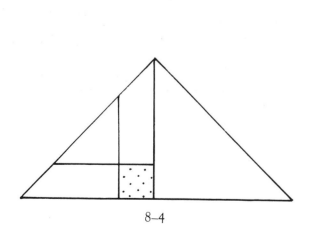

8–4

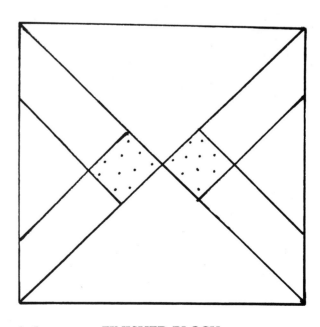

8–5   **FINISHED BLOCK**

Double Flower Garden

53

Multiblock (68 × 86 inches)

9 Multiblock

This quilt is another example of an all-over quilt, and it is fairly easy to make. The Multiblock design was very popular in the 1800s.

YARDAGE

Fabric A	1¾ yards
Fabric B	1½ yards
Fabric C	¾ yard
Fabric D	¾ yard
First border	¾ yard
Second border	1 yard
Third border	1½ yards

CUTTING

Fabric A	twenty-one strips 2½ × 45 inches
Fabric B	eighteen strips 2½ × 45 inches
Fabric C	nine strips 2½ × 45 inches
Fabric D	six strips 2½ × 45 inches
First border	eight strips 3 × 45 inches
Second border	eight strips 4 × 45 inches
Third border	eight strips 5 × 45 inches

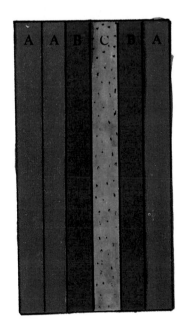

9–1

SEWING DIRECTIONS

We will be sewing our strips into sheets. Refer to 9–1; sew your strips together along their lengths in the following order: A A B C B A. Repeat two more times. Press flat. Pin a small sheet of paper to these sheets, and label it sheet 1. Set aside.

Next sew three sheets each in the same way described above.

Three of sheet 2: D A A B C B

Three of sheet 3: B D A A B C

See 9–2 and 9–3. Press each sheet and label.

For the next step, first look at 9–4, then measure down 2½ inches from the top of your sewn sheet 1. Make sure that the line you just marked is 2½ inches all the way across the top of the sheet. Now cut across that line. You should now have a strip of squares. Continue to measure and cut strips until you have completely cut both of your sheet 1's. Stack these in a pile and mark them with the sheet 1 label.

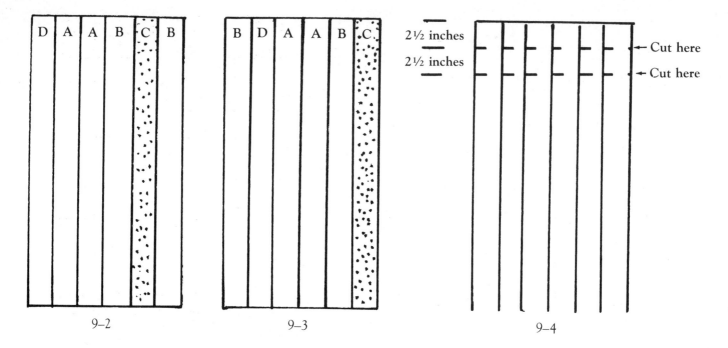

9–2   9–3   9–4

Cut the rest of the sheets, and stack them, making sure to label each stack for easy identification.

The sheets were cut horizontally, and now you will sew them together vertically. Use 9–5 as a guide. The letters indicated in 9–5 are the last three blocks of each strip. Sew together all the strips as shown. These sewn sheets will form the right and left halves of your blocks.

Sew your half blocks together as indicated in 9–6. Repeat twenty-four times. Press your completed blocks flat.

Your quilt top will consist of six rolls. Each roll will have four blocks in it.

Add borders as directed (p. 14).

9–5

Sew blocks together

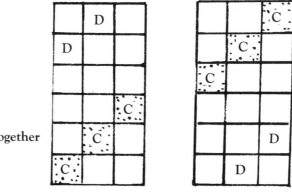

FINISHED BLOCKS

9–6

56

Multiblock

Patience Corner (53×71 inches)

10 Patience Corner

After the Amish Bar Quilt, this is the second easiest quilt in this book. Diaries dated in the 1840s contain stories of young girls who were not allowed to play until they cut out their daily number of pieces, which would be sewn together that evening, or sometime soon, to form a quilt. We also have historical evidence that fathers and sons would help cut out templates and even do some sewing.

YARDAGE

Fabric A	¾ yard
Fabric B	¾ yard
Fabric C	1¾ yards
First border	¾ yard
Second border	1 yard
Third border	1½ yards

CUTTING

Fabric A	four strips 4 × 45 inches
Fabric B	four strips 4 × 45 inches
Fabric C	twenty-two strips 2½ × 45 inches
First border	eight strips 3 × 45 inches
Second border	eight strips 4 × 45 inches
Third border	eight strips 5 × 45 inches

SEWING DIRECTIONS

Place a fabric A strip faceup on your sewing machine. Lay a fabric C strip facedown on the machine, and sew the length. Repeat for a total of four times. Press the fabric open.

Sew the fabric B strips the same way four times. Press open.

Measure down the sewn strips 4 inches and cut (see 10–1), continuing to measure down the length of the strip and cutting every 4 inches. Repeat until all strips are cut. You will need forty from fabric A and forty from fabric B.

Lay a fabric C strip faceup on your machine. Place a block cut from fabric A face down with the attached fabric C strip to the top. (See 10–2.) Sew the length, butting in new blocks until all the fabric A

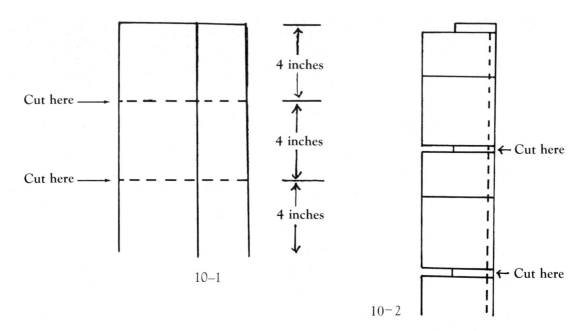

Cut here →

Cut here →

4 inches

4 inches

4 inches

10–1

← Cut here

← Cut here

10–2

blocks are sewn to strips from fabric C. Press flat, and cut according to the illustration.

Sew fabric B blocks the same way. Press flat and cut.

You should have eighty small blocks, and we will pair these off.

Place a block with a fabric A square faceup on your sewing machine. Make sure the fabric A block is in the upper left corner. Lay a block with a fabric B square facedown, having the fabric B square in the lower right corner. Sew the length. Repeat for a total of forty times. (See 10–3.)

Lay your newly sewn rectangle faceup on your machine, having the fabric A block in the upper right corner. Lay another rectangle facedown with the fabric A block in the lower left corner. Sew the length; repeat twenty times. (See 10–4.) Press your finished block flat.

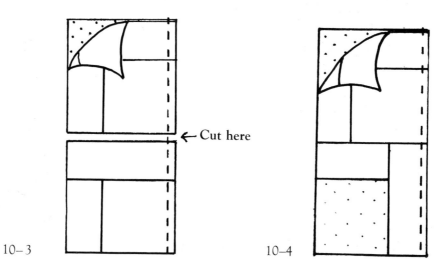

← Cut here

10–3

10–4

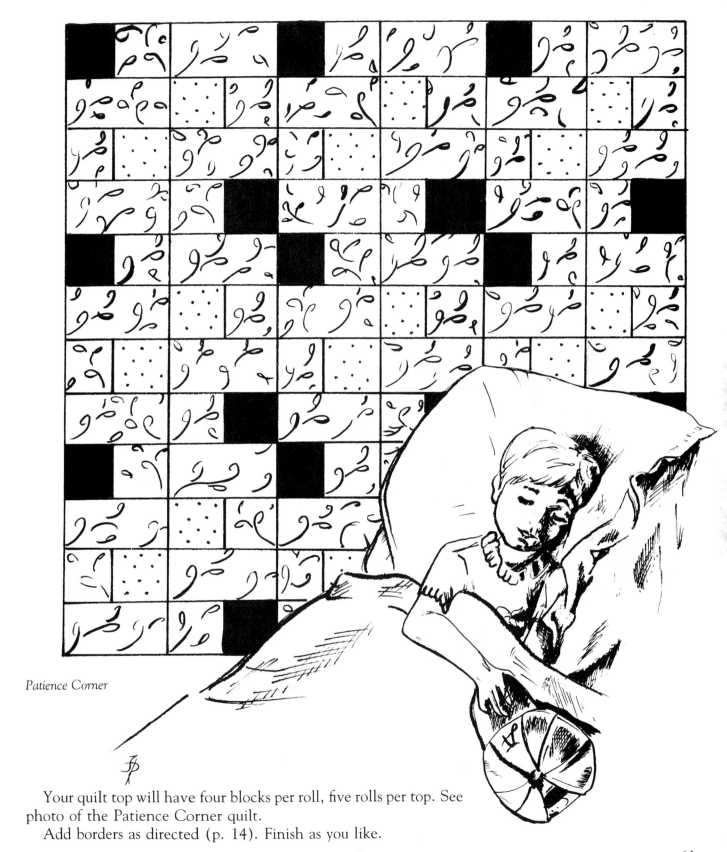

Patience Corner

Your quilt top will have four blocks per roll, five rolls per top. See photo of the Patience Corner quilt.

Add borders as directed (p. 14). Finish as you like.

Shadowed Windows (62 × 73 inches)

11 Shadowed Windows

Children enjoy this quilt, and it is so easy to make that an older child could do it. When looking at this quilt, you can readily envision a fellow quilter studying a window and allowing her imagination to go wild. Although this design is original, it resembles the traditional Log Cabin American quilt which dates to the 1700s.

YARDAGE

Very dark color (center square)	¾ yard
Dark fabric	¾ yard
Medium fabric	¾ yard
Light fabric	1 yard
First border	¾ yard
Second border	1 yard
Third border	1½ yards

CUTTING

Very dark fabric (center square)	three strips 5½ × 45 inches
Dark fabric	seven strips 2½ × 45 inches
Medium fabric	nine strips 2½ × 45 inches
Light fabric	twelve strips 2½ × 45 inches
First border	eight strips 3 × 45 inches
Second border	eight strips 4 × 45 inches
Third border	eight strips 5 × 45 inches

SEWING DIRECTIONS

Sew the length of your center square strip and your dark color strip with right sides together. Do this with all three of your center strips. (See 11–1.) Press seams open.

Measure 5½ inches down, making sure your squares measure 5½ inches all the way across. Cut. (See 11–2.) Cut all your center strips until you have twenty sewn blocks.

11–1

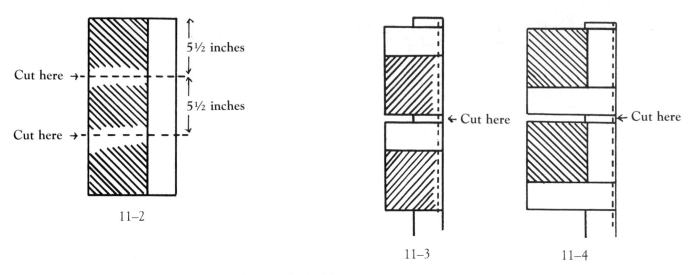

11–2

5½ inches

5½ inches

Cut here →

Cut here →

← Cut here

← Cut here

11–3

11–4

Place a dark fabric strip faceup on your sewing machine. Lay a sewn square with the attached dark fabric strip towards the top, facedown, and sew the length, butting in the center blocks until all have been attached to a dark strip. Cut them apart, and press seams open. (See 11–3.)

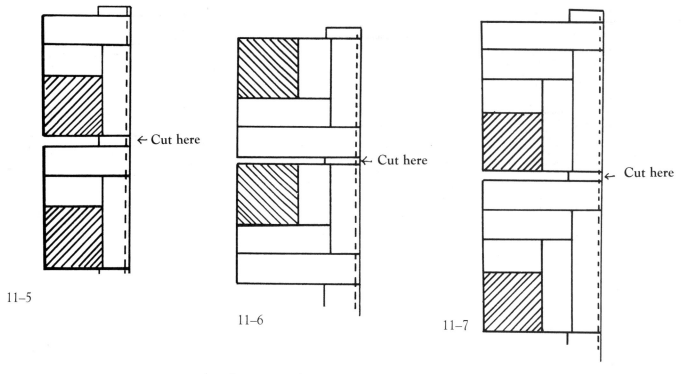

← Cut here

← Cut here

← Cut here

11–5

11–6

11–7

Lay a medium-color strip faceup on the machine. Lay your block facedown on your strip, with the center square in the upper left corner. (See 11–4.) Sew the length, butting in blocks until they've all been attached to a medium-color strip. Cut them apart, and press seams open.

Shadowed Windows

65

Still working with our medium colored strips, lay one faceup on your sewing machine. Lay your block facedown on the strip with the center square in the lower left corner. Sew the length, butting in new blocks until all blocks have been attached for the second time to a medium-color strip. (See 11–5.) Cut apart and press seams open.

Lay a light-color strip faceup on your machine. Lay your blocks facedown on your strip, with the center square in the upper left corner. Sew the length, butting in new blocks until all have been added to a light-color strip. (See 11–6.) Cut them apart, and press seams open.

This will be the last strip added to our blocks. After we add this strip, we're done with our blocks.

Lay a light-color strip faceup on your sewing machine. Lay your block facedown on your strip with the center square in the lower left corner. Sew down the length, butting in more blocks until all blocks have been added, a second time, to a light strip. (See 11–7.) Cut them apart and press seams open. (See 11–8.)

Sew your blocks together, so that your quilt top will have five rolls with four blocks in each roll.

Add borders according to directions under Speed Techniques (p. 14). Finish as you like.

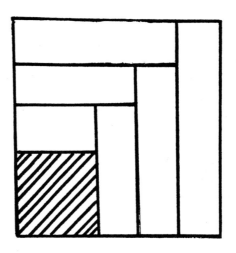

11–8   **FINISHED BLOCK**

12   High and Low

You probably should not make High and Low your first project, but you could try it as a second or third quilt to add to your repertoire. It's a perfect example of a pieced quilt. Up until the early 1700s, all pieced quilts were tied. The Leven's Hall quilt, made in England around 1708, is the first known to combine quilting and pieced work.

YARDAGE

Fabric A	3½ yards
Fabric B	5½ yards

CUTTING

Fabric A	thirty strips 1½ × 45 inches
Fabric B	thirty-six strips 1½ × 45 inches
Fabric A	two strips 3½ × 45 inches
Fabric B	two strips 3½ × 45 inches
Fabric B	four strips 6½ × 45 inches
Fabric A (First border)	eight strips 3 × 45 inches
Fabric B (Second border)	eight strips 4 × 45 inches

SEWING DIRECTIONS

1. Sew the lengths of three 1½-inch fabric A strips together. Press and repeat four times in all. Now attach a 6½-inch fabric B strip to the 1½-inch sewn strips. Repeat four times in all. Press seams open, and set aside.

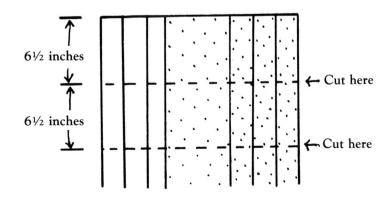

6½ inches

6½ inches

← Cut here

← Cut here

12–1

High and Low (60 × 72 inches)

Sew the lengths of three 1½-inch fabric B strips together. Repeat four times in all. Attach to the 6½-inch fabric B sewn strip. (See 12–1.) Press. Measure down 6½ inches and cut. Do this twenty-four times, using all four sewn sheets. Set aside.

2. Sew three 1½-inch fabric A strips together, sewing them lengthwise. Do this four times. Press, measure down 6½ inches, and cut. Repeat twenty-four times in all. (See 12–2.) Set aside.

3. Sew three 1½-inch fabric B strips together, sewing the length. Repeat four times in all. Press and measure down 6½ inches, and cut twenty-four times in all. (See 12–2.) Set aside.

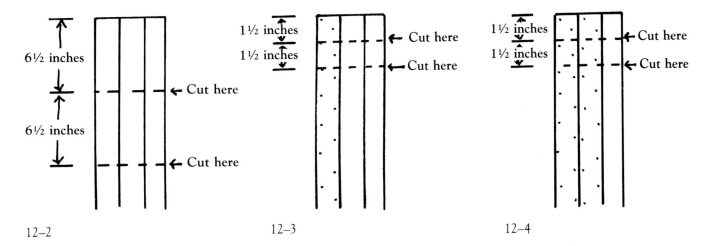

12–2   12–3   12–4

4. Sew a 1½-inch fabric B strip to a 1½-inch fabric A strip, then add a second 1½-inch fabric A strip to the just finished fabric A strip. (See 12–3.) Repeat twice. Press, measure down 1½ inches, and cut. Repeat forty-eight times in all.

5. Sew two 1½-inch fabric B strips together, then sew a 1½-inch fabric A strip to the just sewn 1½-inch fabric B strips. (See 12–4.) Press, measure down 1½ inches, and cut. Do this forty-eight times in all.

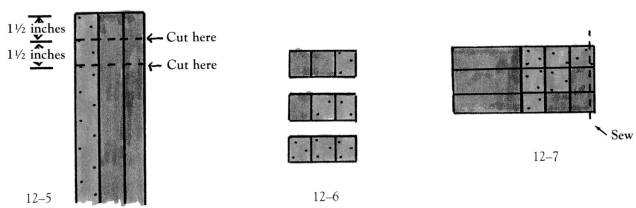

12–5   12–6   12–7

6. Sew three 1½-inch fabric B strips together. Repeat a second time. Press, measure down 1½ inches, and cut. Do this forty-eight times. (See 12–5.)

7. Using the pieces from steps 4, 5, and 6, construct a block that looks like 12–6. Make forty-eight blocks in all. Press.

8. Using the pieces from steps 2 and 7, sew them together as shown in 12–7. Do this twenty-four times in all.

9. Place a 3½-inch fabric A strip faceup on your sewing machine. Lay a piece from step 8 facedown with the pieced block to the far left. Sew down the short end, butt in new pieces until all twenty-four pieces have been added to a 3½-inch fabric A strip. Cut where indicated in 12–8.

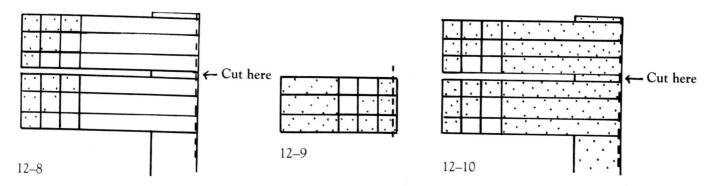

← Cut here

12–8

12–9

← Cut here

12–10

10. Using a piece from step 3 and another from step 7, sew as shown in 12–9.

11. Place a 3½-inch fabric B strip faceup on your machine. Lay a piece from step 10 facedown. Sew as directed in step 9, using 12–10 as a guide.

12. Sew the pieces from step 9 and step 11 to the pieces from step 1. Your finished block should look like 12–11.

13. Sew the blocks together in whatever appealing way you like. Add borders (see p. 14), and finish as you will.

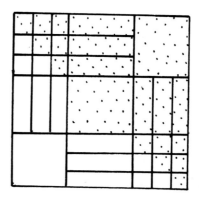

12–11   **FINISHED BLOCK**

13 Quick Fan

This is not the easiest quilt, but it is certainly not the most exacting either. I created the Quick Fan so that I could use up leftover strips. It makes a lovely lap quilt. The true Fan Quilt is a sister to the Dresden Plate quilt, which dates back to the early 1800s.

YARDAGE

Ten different colors (2½ yards total)	¼ yard each
Solid color	1 yard
Light color	2 yards
Backing	6 yards
First border	¾ yard
Second border	1 yard
Third border	1½ yards

CUTTING

Ten different colors	three strips 2½ × 45 inches each
Solid color	three strips 10½ × 45 inches
Light color	three strips 7 × 45 inches
Light color	fourteen strips 2½ × 45 inches
First border	eight strips 3 × 45 inches
Second border	eight strips 4 × 45 inches
Third border	eight strips 5 × 45 inches

SEWING DIRECTIONS

After cutting your ten different colors, divide them into two equal piles—with the first pile having fabrics A to E and the second pile, fabrics F to J. Start with the first pile. Take fabric strip A, and sew it lengthwise with fabric strip B with right sides together. (See 13–1.) We're going to chain-stitch, so you'll want to review Speed Techniques discussed earlier. Continue sewing the same way until both strips A and B are sewn together. Then cut them free from the sewing machine and free from each other. Now we'll begin to build on these sewn strips by adding fabric strip C to the fabric B side of your sewn strips. Sew right sides together, stitching the length of the strips. Add strip C to your

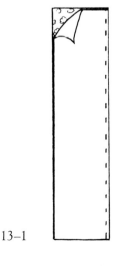

13–1

Sew strips A and B together

73

High and Low

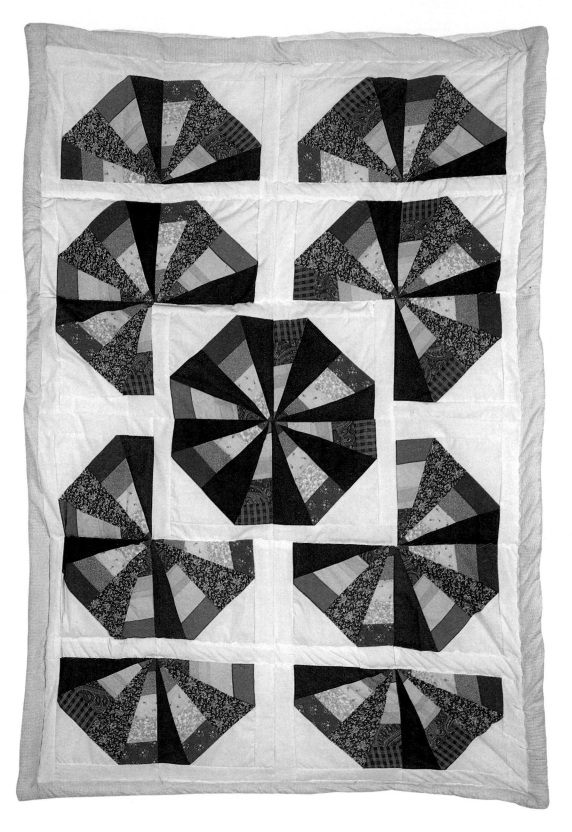

Quick Fan (62 × 72 inches)

other sewn strips as well. Continue building on your sewn strips in the same way until you've added the strips D and E. (See 13–2, 13–3, and 13–4.) Press your sewn sheets and set aside.

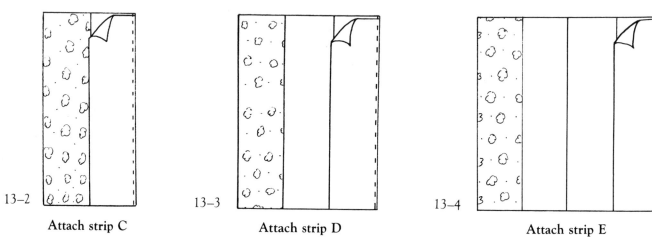

13–2 Attach strip C

13–3 Attach strip D

13–4 Attach strip E

With strips from the second pile, fabrics F to J, sew just as we did the strips from the first pile. Starting with fabric strips F and G, build on these. Press.

Now you have a total of six sewn sheets, three from each pile, all pressed and ready to cut.

Measure down 5 inches on your sewn strips and cut across. (See 13–5.) You'll get eight 5-inch-by-10½-inch rectangles from each sewn sheet. You'll need twenty-four 5-inch-by-10½-inch rectangles in all.

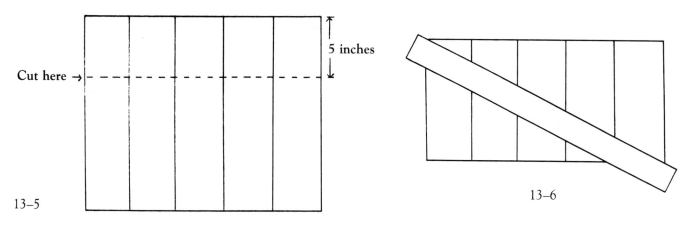

Cut here →

5 inches

13–5

13–6

Take your rectangle strips (which became stripes), place a ruler or your Plexiglas on the upper left corner and bring the opposite end of your ruler down to the lower right corner. Then, using your rotary cutter, cut so that you have two triangles. (See 13–6.) Cut all twenty-four rectangles this way, so that you end up with a total of forty-eight striped triangles. Set them aside, keeping them in the two separate piles.

We're going to work with the 10½-inch-by-45-inch solid fabric.

Lay it on your cutting mat, and measure down 5 inches from the top and cut. (See 13–7.) Cut a total of twenty-four solid rectangles, measuring 5 inches by 10½ inches. Now we're going to cut the solid rectangles into triangles. Place your ruler or Plexiglas in the upper right corner, and bring the opposite end of your ruler down to the lower left corner. Using the rotary cutter, cut to make two triangles. (See 13–8; notice that this is opposite of the way we cut the striped triangles.) When finished, you will have a total of forty-eight triangles.

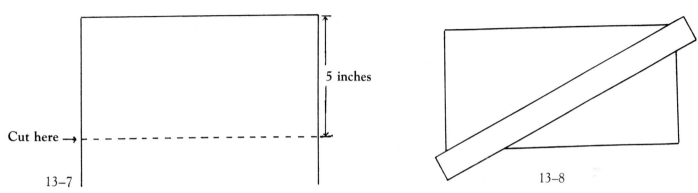

5 inches

Cut here →

13–7

13–8

To the left of your sewing machine, place the first pile of striped triangles, then solid triangles, and finally striped triangles. By laying them down this way, you will be able to sew faster.

Place a solid triangle, right side up. With the angled side towards your needle, place a striped triangle from the fist pile facedown, on the solid triangle. Sew down the angled edge. (See 13–9.) Chain-stitch your next triangle into the sewing machine, using one solid on the bottom and one striped from the second pile. Continue sewing the triangles the same way until all triangles are sewn in pairs, alternating between the first and second piles. When you finish, you'll have forty-eight sets of triangles. Cut triangles free from each other, and press them open.

Place a sewn triangle faceup on your sewing machine. Place another sewn triangle facedown on top of it, and sew the straight edge. (See 13–10.) Butt in until all sets are sewn together. You'll have twenty-four "fans" when you are finished.

Take the three 7-inch-by-45-inch light-color strips, and measure down 7 inches and cut across so that you'll have a 7-inch-by-7-inch square. Now cut diagonally to form two triangles. You'll get five 7-inch-by-7-inch squares from each strip. You will need to cut twelve squares total, twenty-four triangles in all.

Take a triangle, and sew it to the top of your fan. Once you look at 13–11, you will see what I mean by "sewing it to the top." After having attached all the triangles to the top of the fans, press them open.

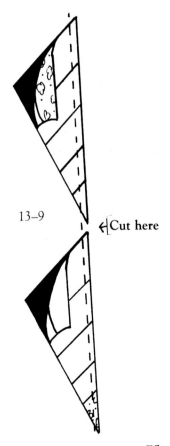

13–9

←Cut here

Quick Fan

Place a 2½-inch-by-45-inch light-color strip faceup on your sewing machine. Lay a fan facedown with the just-added triangle at the top. (See 13–12.) Butt in your fans until all the fans have been added to a strip. Cut them free as indicated in 13–12.

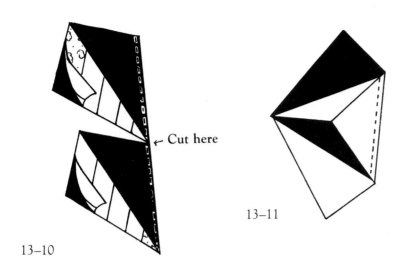

← Cut here

13–11

13–10

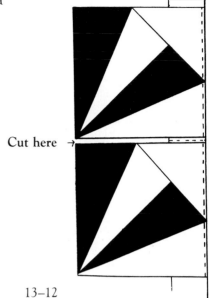

Cut here →

13–12

Lay a 2½-inch-by-45 inch light-color strip faceup on your sewing machine. Lay a fan facedown, only this time with the triangle at the bottom. (See 13–13.) This will frame two sides of your square with a light color, allowing your fan to stand out. Continue butting in squares until all squares have been added to a strip. Cut squares as shown in 13–13. Press your squares flat.

This pattern was designed with the idea of having four squares across and six rolls deep. You may place all the fans going to the right *or* to the left. You could also place them as shown in the photo on p. 72, or vary the number of fans and have, say, five across and four or five down as shown in the drawing on p. 76.

Sew on borders, following directions under Speed Techniques (p. 14). Finish as you like.

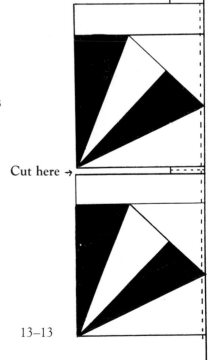

Cut here →

13–13

Flower Basket

78

14 Flower Basket

This quilt, while not hard to make, does require care when piecing and sewing the handles of the flower baskets together. I love all the different printed fabrics, but did you know that printed fabric dates from the 4th century? Modern archaeologists have discovered wooden blocks with carved designs used for printing on fabric with vegetable dyes. They could print on the material using more than one color at a time. With these print blocks, archaeologists also found garments that showed how the patterns were used. Most fabric prints were created this way until the 1740s.

YARDAGE

Fabric A	2½ yards
Fabric B	1½ yards
Fabric C (large flower print)	¾ yard
First border	¾ yard
Second border	¾ yard
Third border	1¼ yards

CUTTING

Fabric A (cut four on the diagonal and cut one diagonally both ways [crisscross])	nine strips 12½ × 12½ inches
Fabric B (cut on the diagonal for ten triangles)	five strips 8 × 8 inches
Fabric C (cut on the diagonal for ten triangles)	five strips 8 × 8 inches
Fabric A	five strips 2½ × 45 inches
First border	six strips 3 × 45 inches
Second border	six strips 4 × 45 inches
Third border	seven strips 5 × 45 inches

Graph and cut out fifty-six squares 3 × 3 inches from Fabrics A and B (fourteen across and four down); you'll need one hundred triangle-squares.

Flower Basket (51 × 64 inches)

SEWING DIRECTIONS

With this quilt, you will have an extra basket square, so choose your best nine for the body of your quilt. You could use the extra one for a pillow or a square in a sampler quilt.

1. Sew a large triangle from fabric B to a large triangle from fabric C. Sew them together on the diagonal. Repeat ten times. Press open and set aside. This is the base of your basket with flowers.

2. Sew and cut your grafted 3-inch squares as directed in the section on speed techniques under Half-Square Triangles. You'll need one hundred triangle-squares. Press them open, and set aside twenty triangle-squares for the base of your basket. Also set aside forty for the left side of the basket handle. This will leave forty triangle-squares for the basket's right side.

3. Place on the triangle-square faceup on your sewing machine with fabric B in the upper right corner. Lay another triangle-square facedown with fabric B in the upper left corner as shown in 14–1. Repeat twenty times.

4. Place a piece from step 3 faceup on your machine with fabric B placed in the upper right corner. Lay another sewn set from step 3 facedown with fabric B in the upper left corner. (See 14–2.) Repeat ten times in all. Press open.

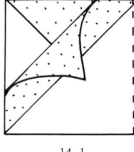

14–1

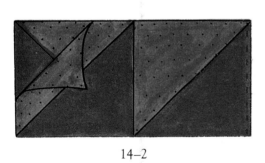

14–2

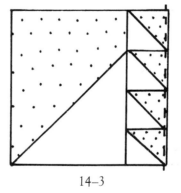

14–3

14–4

5. Lay your large triangle-square from step 1 faceup on your sewing machine with fabric B in the upper left corner. Place your newly sewn strip from step 4 facedown with fabric B in the upper right corner. (See 14–3.) Repeat ten times. Press flat and set aside.

The first few times I made this pattern, my strip was a little long. Check to see if it fits. If it is too long, enlarge your seams, and if it is too short, make them narrower.

6. Follow directions for step 3, except change the direction of fabric B. For the bottom triangle-square, have fabric B in the upper left top with a triangle-square with fabric B on the upper right on top. Sew and repeat twenty times. (See 14–4.) Press open.

7. Follow directions for step 4, changing fabric B to the upper left corner for the bottom strip. Top it with a strip having fabric B in the upper right. Sew and repeat ten times. (See 14–5.) Press open.

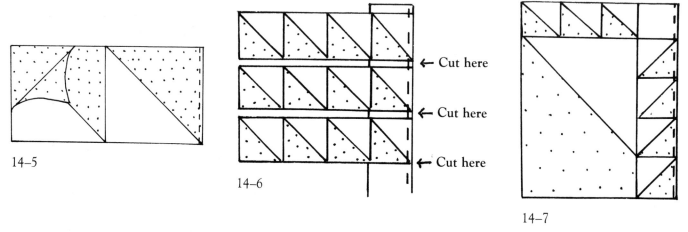

14–5

14–6

← Cut here

← Cut here

← Cut here

14–7

8. Lay one 2½-inch strip faceup on the sewing machine. Lay your strip from step 7 facedown with fabric A in the lower left corner. (See 14–6.) Repeat ten times. Cut as indicated and press.

9. Take the large triangle-square from step 5, and place it faceup on the machine with the attached small triangle-square to the top. Place your strip from step 8 facedown with the solid square at the top. (See 14–7.) Check to see if the strip fits. Repeat ten times. Press, square off, and set aside.

10. Take your remaining 2½-inch strips, and cut them into twenty 8-inch lengths and ten 2½-inch-by-2½-inch squares. Sew ten of your 8-inch lengths as seen in 14–8. And sew ten as shown in 14–9.

Take your strips from 14–9, and sew one of your 2½-inch squares to the triangle-square end so that it will look like 14–10. Repeat this a total of ten times. Open and press all twenty sewn strips.

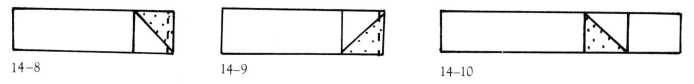

14–8

14–9

14–10

11. Lay the square from step 9 faceup on your sewing machine with fabric B on the upper right. Place a strip from 14–8 with the small triangle-square at the top. Sew the length and repeat ten times. (See 14–11.)

12. Lay the square faceup on your machine with fabric B in the lower right corner. Place your strip from 14–10 facedown with the small triangle-square to the bottom. Sew the length and repeat ten times. Press.

13. Assemble your quilt as shown in 14–13, using the fabric squares from fabric A. Working diagonally, sew your rolls using the solid shapes from fabric A. Add borders as directed in Speed Techniques (p. 14), and finish as you wish.

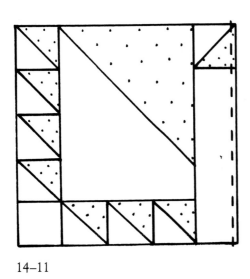

14–11

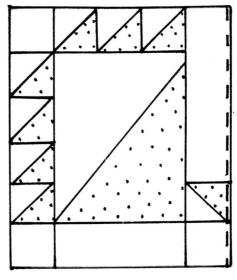

14–12   **FINISHED BLOCK**

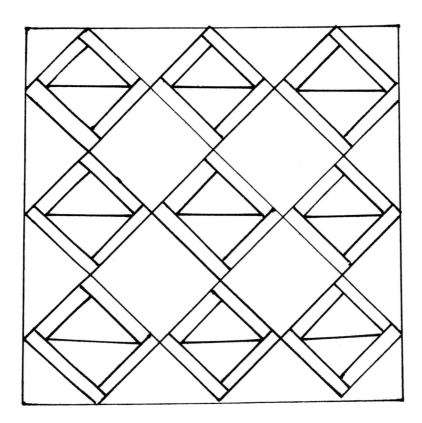

14–13   **FINISHED QUILT WITHOUT BORDERS**

Indian Homeland (71 × 71 inches)

15 Indian Homeland

Indian Homeland is a lovely quilt that's very easy to make. Strip quilters owe great thanks to the originators of Seminole piecing—sewing fabric together, then cutting it, to form a design. The Seminoles, removed to Oklahoma in the 1840s, and the Black Seminoles, who settled in Florida, spread this technique in the early to mid-1800s, along the southern American territories into Mexico.

YARDAGE

Fabric A	3 yards
Fabric B	3 yards

CUTTING

Fabric A (cut on the diagonal)	six strips 12 × 12 inches
Fabric A	one strip 6 × 45 inches
Fabric A	one strip 6 × 6 inches
Fabric A (cut one strip into two 18-inch lengths and two 4½-inch lengths)	three strips 4½ × 45 inches
Fabric B (cut on the diagonal)	six strips 12 × 12 inches
Fabric B	four strips 6 × 45 inches
Fabric B (cut one strip into two 18-inch lengths and one 4½-inch length)	four strips 4½ × 45 inches
Fabric A (first border)	eight strips 4 × 45 inches
Fabric B (second border)	eight strips 4 × 45 inches

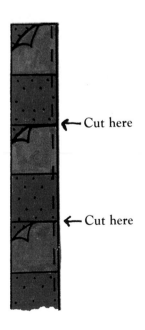

← Cut here

← Cut here

15–1

SEWING DIRECTIONS

1. Sew one fabric A and one fabric B triangle together on the bias. Repeat twelve times in all. Press flat and set aside.

2. Sew the length of a fabric A 6-inch strip to a fabric B 6-inch strip right sides together. Measure down 6 inches from the top of your sewn strip and cut. You'll need to attach the 6-inch-by-6-inch square to the top of a fabric B 6-inch strip in order to get your full eight twin blocks.

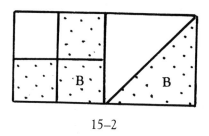

15–2

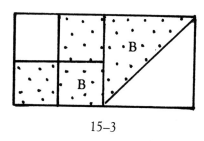

15–3

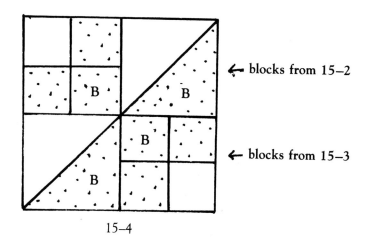

← blocks from 15–2

← blocks from 15–3

15–4

After cutting them free from the strips, press flat. Lay a 6-inch fabric B strip facedown on your machine. Lay a twin block faceup with the fabric A block at the top, butt in new blocks to the strip until they all have been attached. Cut where indicated in 15–1. Press.

3. Sew four of your triangle-squares from step 1 onto four of the blocks from step 2 as shown in 15–2. Sew another set of four as shown in 15–3.

4. Sew your pieces from step 3 (see 15–4). Repeat for a total of four times. Press and set aside.

5. Sew one combination as seen in 15–5 from the 4½-inch-by-18-inch strips. Measure down 4½ inches from the top and cut. You now have the middle strip for building the blocks. Repeat four times.

6. Place your fabric A 4½-inch-by-18-inch strip faceup on your sewing machine. Lay your center strip (see previous step) facedown, and sew the length. Use your other 4½-inch-by-45-inch strip for the remaining middle strips. Attach the 4½-inch fabric B strip in the same way to the other side of the strip of blocks so that you complete four blocks that look like 15–6.

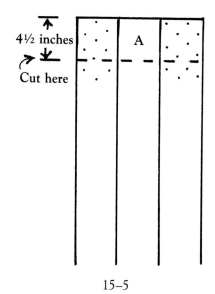

4½ inches

Cut here

A

15–5

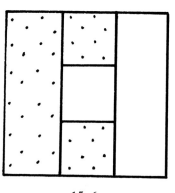

15–6

7. Attach your block from step 6 to the triangle-square from step 1 as shown in 15–7. Repeat a second time. Sew a set of two as shown in 15–8.

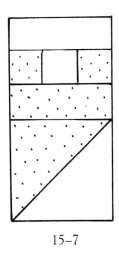

15–7

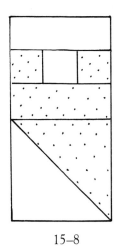

15–8

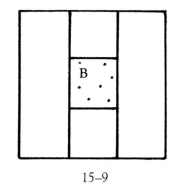

15–9

8. Using your 4½-inch-by-4½-inch blocks of fabrics A and B as well as your 4½-inch-by-45-inch strip, construct a center block as shown in 15–9.

9. To complete the construction of your quilt top, look at the Indian Homeland photo. Add borders as directed (p. 14).

Chain Link (60 × 74 inches)

16 Chain Link

The Chain Link is not a difficult quilt. While I was not able to trace its history, I am sure it must have been designed by someone who loved puzzles. It did indeed take me some time to discover an easier way than the traditional one to put this quilt together.

YARDAGE

Fabric A	1¾ yards
Fabric B	1½ yards
Fabric C	1½ yards
First border	1 yard

CUTTING

Fabric A	five strips 2½ × 45 inches
Fabric A	nine strips 4½ × 45 inches
Fabric B	seventeen strips 2½ × 45 inches
Fabric C	two strips 2½ × 45 inches
Fabric C	three strips 4½ × 45 inches
Fabric C	three strips 9 × 45 inches

16–1

SEWING DIRECTIONS

1. Place a 4½-inch strip of fabric A faceup on your sewing machine. Lay a fabric B strip facedown, and sew the length. Repeat nine times in all. (See 16–1.)

2. Measure down your sewn strip 4½ inches, and cut. Continue to measure and cut down the length of the strip. Do this for all nine strips. You'll need eighty of these blocks. (See 16–2.) Press the seams open, and set the blocks aside.

3. Place a 2½-inch fabric A strip faceup on your machine. Lay a fabric B strip facedown, and sew the length. Repeat three times in all.

4. Measure down your sewn strip 2½ inches and cut. Continue down the length of the strip. Repeat with three strips. You'll need forty of these blocks. Press the seams open.

5. Place a large block from step 2 faceup on your sewing machine with the fabric A strip to the left. Lay a small block from step 4 facedown with the fabric B to the top. (See 16–3.) Sew the length. Repeat forty times in all.

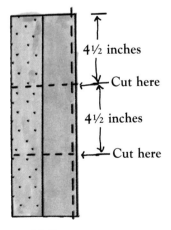

4½ inches
Cut here
4½ inches
Cut here

16–2

CHAIN LINK WORKSHEET

Pin a small swatch of fabric by the assigned letter.

A

B

C

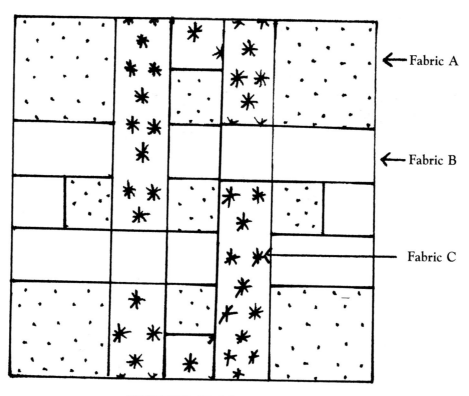

FINISHED BLOCK

6. Take your newly sewn piece from step 5, and lay it faceup with the large block to the left. Place another large block facedown on the small block, having the fabric B to the far right. (See 16–4.) Repeat forty times in all. Press the seams flat, and set aside. (See 16–4.)

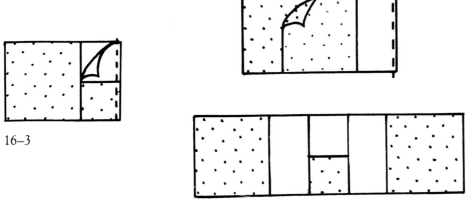

16–3

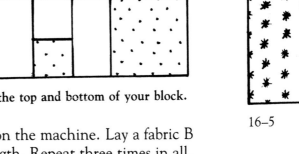

16–4   This will be the top and bottom of your block.

16–5

7. Place the 9-inch fabric C faceup on the machine. Lay a fabric B 2½-inch strip facedown, and sew the length. Repeat three times in all. (See 16–5.)

8. Place your newly sewn combination from step 7 faceup on your machine with the 9-inch strip to the left. Place your 4½-inch strip of fabric C facedown, and sew the length. Repeat three times in all. (See 16–6.)

9. Measure down your newly sewn combination 2½ inches, and cut all the way across. Continue down the strip. Repeat to create three strips in all. You'll need forty of these cut pieces. Press flat. (See 16–7.)

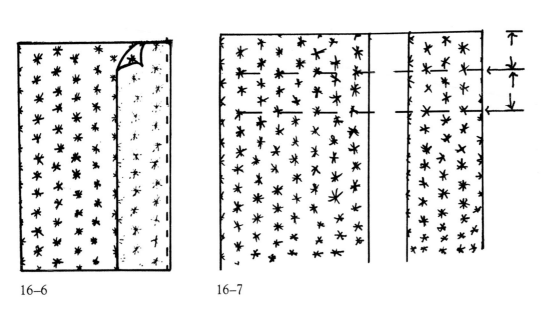

16–6   16–7   16–8

Chain Link
92

10. Take your sewn pieces from step 6. Lay one of these strips faceup on your sewing machine as shown in 16–8. Lay a strip from step 9 facedown, with the 9-inch section to the top. Match the fabric B seams where needed. (See 16–9.) Sew the length. Repeat forty times in all. Press the seams flat, and set aside. These pieces will be the top and bottom of your block.

11. Sew a combination of strips as seen in 16–10 out of the 2½-inch strips. Repeat a second time.

12. Measure down your sewn combination 2½ inches, and cut all the way across. You will need twenty of these cut pieces from the two-combination sheets. Press flat. This is a joining strip. (See 16–10.)

13. Place a piece from step 10 faceup on your machine with the newly attached fabric C strip to the right. Lay a joining strip from step 12 facedown. Sew the length, matching the fabric B seams where possible. (See 16–11.) Repeat twenty times in all.

14. Place a piece from step 10 faceup on your machine, with the fabric C strip to the right. Lay a piece with an attached joining strip facedown, matching the fabric B seams where possible. Sew the length, repeat twenty times in all. Your block is finished. (See 16–12.)

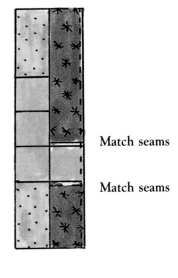

Match seams

Match seams

16–9

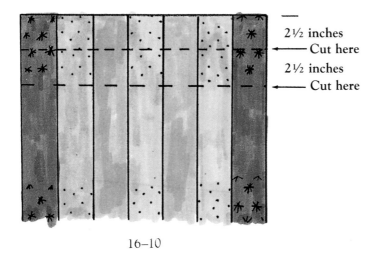

2½ inches
Cut here
2½ inches
Cut here

16–10

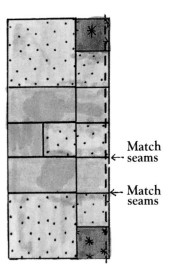

Match seams

Match seams

16–11

15. Your quilt top will have four blocks per roll, with five rolls per quilt top. Attach the border as directed on p. 14. Finish as you like.

93

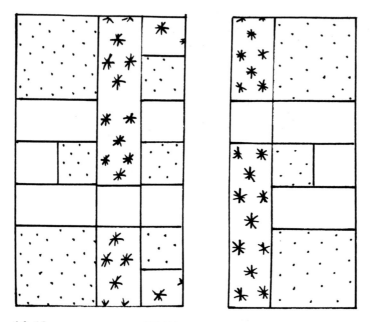

16–12   **FINISHED BLOCKS**

17 Dresden Plate

This is a quilt that's fun to make, and it isn't as hard as it looks. The pattern originally came from a porcelain dinner plate made in Dresden, Germany. Quilts by this name began to appear in the 1800s.

YARDAGE

Fabrics A to E (five different fabrics)	1 yard each
Center of plate	½ yard
Lightweight fabric for lining (cotton) *or* fusible interfacing	3 yards
Background fabric	3½ yards
First border	¾ yard
Second border	1 yard

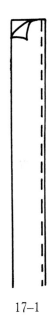

17–1

CUTTING

Fabrics A to E	ten strips 3 × 45 inches each
Center fabric (then cut into twenty 5 × 5-inch squares)	three strips 5 × 45 inches
Lining squares	twelve strips 17 × 17 inches
Background squares	twelve strips 19 × 19 inches
First border	eight strips 3 × 45 inches
Second border	eight strips 4 × 45 inches

SEWING DIRECTIONS

1. Sew the length of your strips, always having the lightest color on the bottom. Repeat twenty-five times in all. (See 17–1.)

2. Cut your sewn strips into 7-inch lengths; you should get at least six rectangles from each sewn strip. (See 17–2.)

3. Photocopy your wedge template, and cut it out. Back it with cardboard. (Or use the idea from helpful hints in the front of the book.) Line up the seam line from the template with the seam of your rectangle and cut along the template. (See 17–3.) Repeat one hundred twenty times in all. Press seams open. You now have two wedges sewn together.

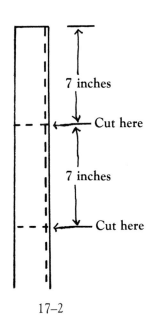

17–2

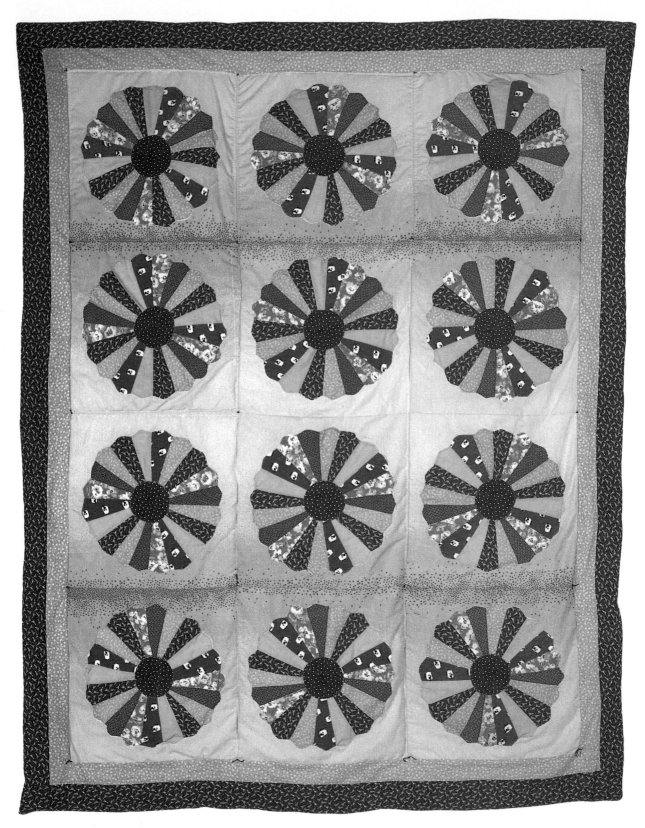

Dresden Plate (64 × 80 inches)

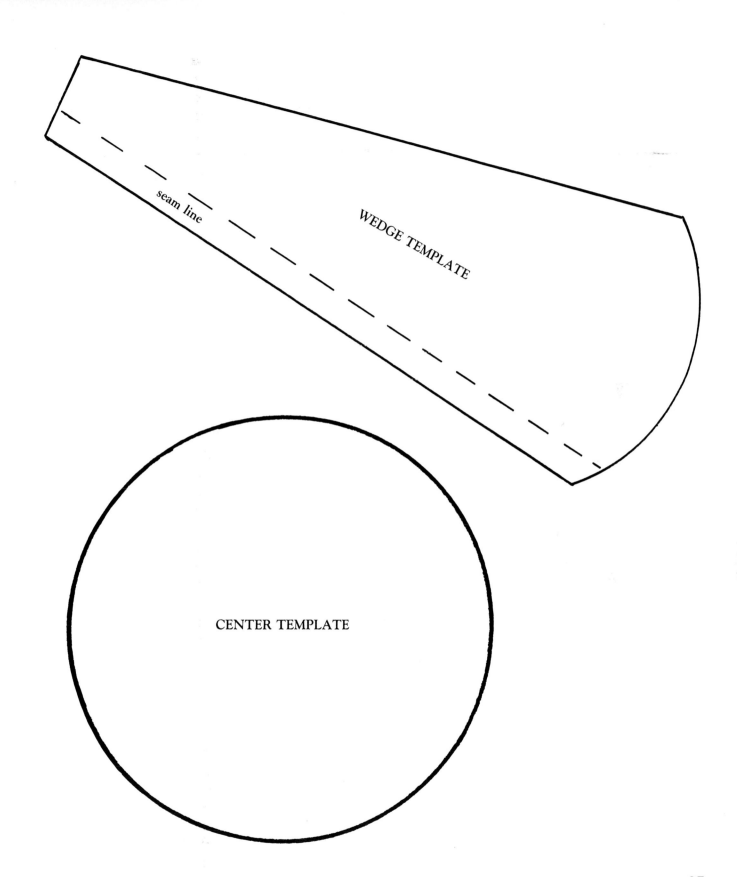

seam line

WEDGE TEMPLATE

CENTER TEMPLATE

17–3

4. Match the wide ends of two different double wedges, and sew them together. (See 17–4.) Repeat sixty times in all. Press flat. You now have four wedges sewn together.

5. Take two of your newly sewn wedges, match the wide ends, and sew the length. (See 17–5.) Repeat twenty-four times in all. You have twelve four-wedge pieces left over. Set them aside for step 7.

6. Take two of your newly sewn wedges, match the wide ends, and sew the length. (See 17–6.) Repeat twelve times in all. Press flat.

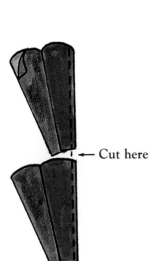

← Cut here

17–4

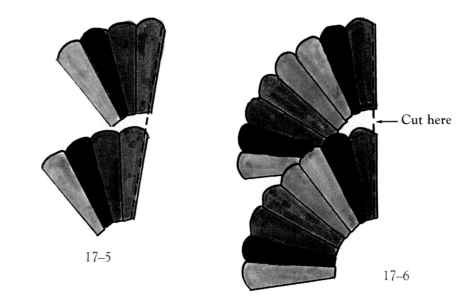

17–5

← Cut here

17–6

7. Take one of your newly sewn wedges, and lay it faceup on your machine. Top it (right sides together) with a four-wedge piece left over from step 5. Match the wide ends, and sew the length.

8. Now let's complete the circle of our plate. Sew the two ends together, matching the wide end. Press on the wrong side, going from the wide end towards the center, and be sure to press the seams in one direction.

9. Place your 17-inch square right side up. Lay one plate facedown, and reduce the length of your stitch to 18 to 20 per inch. Stitch around the outside edge of your plate. Trim with a rotary cutter to within ⅛ inch of your seam. Turn it right side out. Press flat. It must be flat now, or it will not lay flat in your quilt top. Press from the wide end to the narrow. Set aside for step 11. (See 17–7.)

If you use fusible interfacing: Lay fusible interfacing with the glue side faceup and lay your almost completed Dresden plate facedown. Stitch within ¼ inch of the edge through both the fabric and the interfacing all the way around. Trim off extra interfacing, clip curved edges, and

Dresden Plate

turn fabric right side out. Lay your plate on the 17-inch square faceup. Apply a warm iron, and it will stay in place for you to stitch around (no pins are necessary).

10. Make a template from the circle pattern provided. Place two 5-inch-by-5-inch squares, right sides together. Trace your pattern onto the top 5-inch square, and sew with 18 to 20 stitches per inch all the way around. Trim close to the stitching. Pull them apart. (See 17–8.) Cut an X into one of the circles, and turn the right side out. Press flat. Repeat twelve times in all.

11. Set the stitch length on your machine to 12 to 14 stitches per inch. Adjust your stitch to the "blind hem stitch." (You can straight stitch if you don't have a "blind hem stitch" on your machine.)

Pin the circle into the center of your plate, and stitch it in place. Repeat twelve times in all. (See 17–9.)

17–7   Cut out with rotary cutter

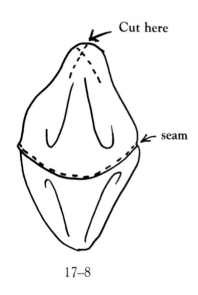

17–8

12. Lay a 19-inch-by-19-inch square faceup. Center a plate on top of the square, faceup, and stitch around the plate, attaching it to the square. Do this twelve times in all.

13. Your quilt top will have three plates per roll and four rolls in all. Attach borders according to directions on pp. 14–15. Finish the quilt as you like.

17–9   **FINISHED BLOCK**

Railroad Crossing (68 × 86 inches)

18 Railroad Crossing

This quilt is slightly more complicated than others in this book, but I really cannot say it is hard. The origin of this quilt dates back to the early 1800s when railroads began to crisscross the United States and Canada.

YARDAGE

Fabrics A to E (five different colors)	⅔ yard each
Fabric F (main color)	3 yards
Fabric G (color used in the crossing)	⅔ yard
First border	¾ yard
Second border	1 yard

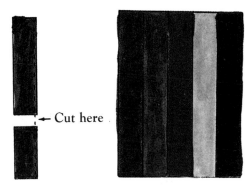

← Cut here

18–1

CUTTING

Fabrics A to E	seven strips 2½ × 45 inches each
Fabric F	eighteen strips 10½ × 10½ inches
Fabric F (then cut on the diagonal into triangles)	five squares 11 × 11 inches
Fabric F (then cut on the diagonal into triangles)	two squares 8 × 8 inches
Fabric G (then cut seven squares on the diagonal into triangles)	twenty-four squares 5½ × 5½ inches
First border	eight strips 3 × 45 inches
Second border	eight strips 4 × 45 inches

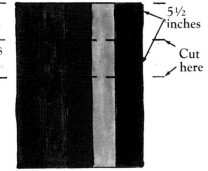

5½ inches

Cut here

SEWING DIRECTIONS

For this pattern, I suggest that you do all your cutting first, mark it, and set it aside.

18–2

Using fabrics A to E, sew a sheet made up of one 2½-inch-by-45-inch strip from each color. (See 18–1.) Arrange colors so that they are pleasing to the eye. Repeat seven times in all. Press seams flat.

Lay your fabric sheet faceup on your cutting mat, measure down 5½ inches from the top, all the way across, and cut. (See 18–2.) Continue all the way down until all sheets are cut. The cut pieces are called *bar strips*.

Place a bar strip faceup on your machine. Lay a triangle from fabric G facedown with the diagonal running from the upper right to the lower left. (See 18–3.) Repeat four times in all.

Working with the same four pieces, lay a bar strip faceup with the newly attached triangle to the far left. Place another triangle from fabric G facedown at the opposite end of your bar strip. Place the triangle down so the diagonal runs from the upper left to the lower right. (See 18–4.) Repeat four times in all.

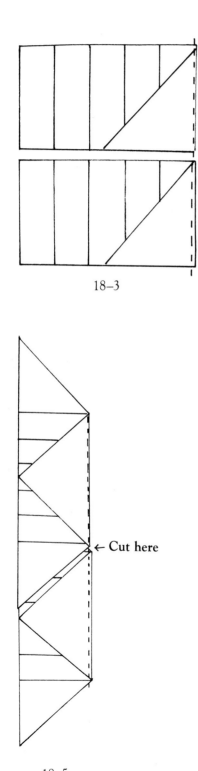

18–3

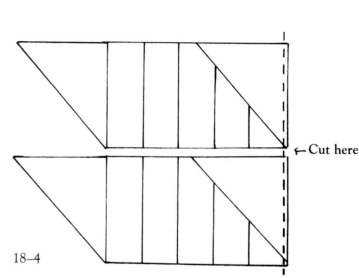

18–4

18–5

Now working with our four triangles that were cut from our 8-inch squares and our sewn bar strips, lay a sewn bar strip, with the attached triangles, vertically on your sewing machine. Place your triangle face-down on the shortest side of the bar strip, and sew. (See 18–5.) (To chain-stitch, lay the top portion of the next piece to be sewn either on top of or below the first sewn piece.) Repeat four times in all.

Press open and set aside; these are the four tip halves of the corners to your quilt top.

Place a 10½-inch square faceup on your machine. Lay a bar strip horizontally facedown, and sew. (See 18–6.) Repeat four times in all.

Attach another bar strip the same way on the opposite side.

Place your square with the attached far strips faceup on your sewing machine so the bar strips are at the sides. Lay a triangle from the 11-inch squares facedown, so the diagonal runs from the upper right corner down to the lower left corner. (See 18–7.) Repeat four times in all.

Place your sewn square faceup on your machine with the newly attached triangle to the far left. Lay a triangle from the 11-inch squares facedown so the diagonal runs from the upper left down to the lower right. (See 18–8.) Repeat four times in all.

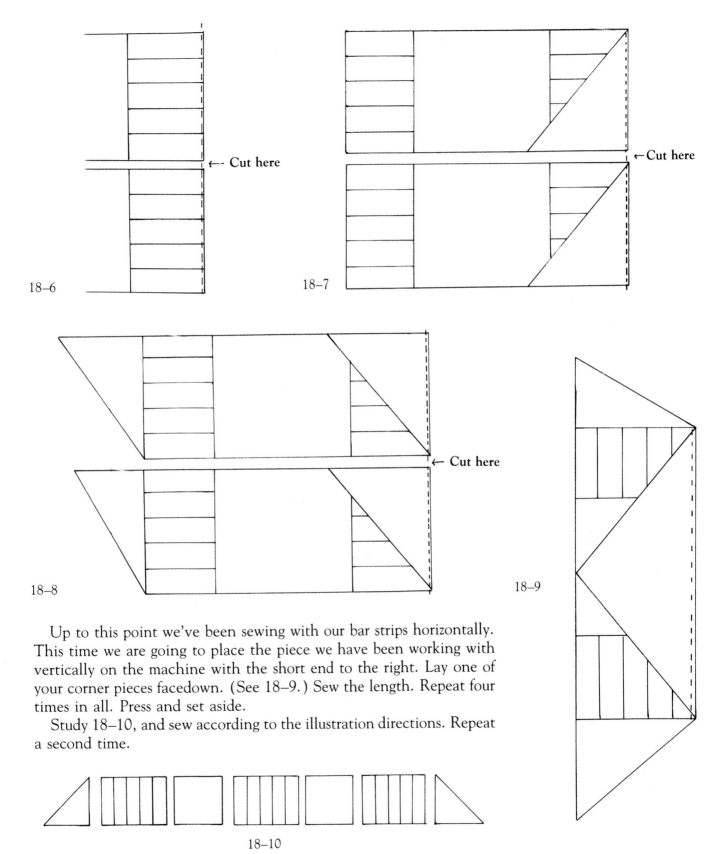

18–6

18–7 ← Cut here

← Cut here

18–8 ← Cut here

18–9

Up to this point we've been sewing with our bar strips horizontally. This time we are going to place the piece we have been working with vertically on the machine with the short end to the right. Lay one of your corner pieces facedown. (See 18–9.) Sew the length. Repeat four times in all. Press and set aside.

Study 18–10, and sew according to the illustration directions. Repeat a second time.

18–10

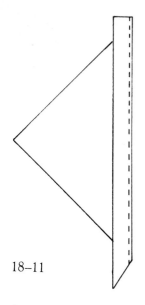

18–11

Match seams as you go

Working with only two corners, place one corner faceup on your machine with the diagonal to the right. Lay the strip you just finished facedown, sewing the top or short end to the right. Sew, matching seams where possible. (See 18–11.) Repeat a second time. This is your built-on-corner, and there are two of these, that we will continue to build on.

Study 18–12 and sew fabric together in the order shown. Repeat a second time.

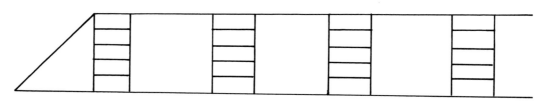

18–12

Place one of your built-on-corners faceup. We will sew on the diagonal. Lay your newly sewn section facedown with the triangle towards the bottom sewn on the shorter side. (See 18–13.) Matching seams as you go, repeat a second time.

Look at 18–14. As you see, you'll need one triangle, four bar strips, and four 5½-inch squares. Sew them together as indicated in the illustration.

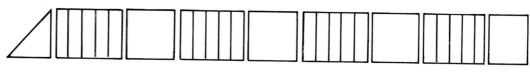

18–14

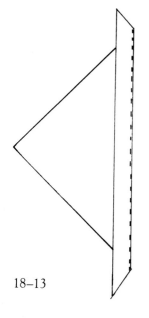

18–13

Match seams as you sew

Place one of your built-on-corners faceup. Again, we'll be sewing on the diagonal. Lay your just-sewn strip facedown with the triangle at the bottom. Sew a second set. (See 18–15.)

Again, refer to the illustration (18–16) for directions. You'll see that we need five bar strips and four 10½-inch squares. Sew according to the illustration, and repeat a second time.

Place one of your built-on-corners faceup on your sewing machine with the diagonal to the right. Lay the strip that you just finished sewing, facedown. Sew, matching seams where possible. (See 18–17.) Repeat a second time.

Railroad Crossing

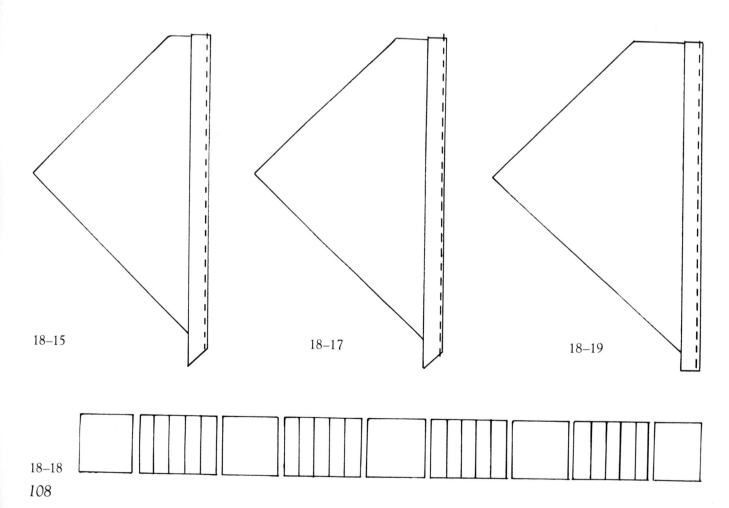

18–16

Now we'll be sewing a joiner strip. Refer to 18–18 to see how to sew the joiner strip. You will need five 5½-inch squares, four bar strips. Do this just once.

Place one built-on-corner faceup on your machine, sewing on the diagonal of the corner. Lay the joiner strips facedown. Sew, matching seams where possible. Do this once. (See 18–19.)

Lay your built-on-corner with the joining strip faceup on your machine. Lay your other built-on-corner facedown, and sew to the joined strip, matching seams where possible. (See 18–20.)

Now, add the two remaining corners, as shown in 18–21.

Attach borders as directed in Speed Techniques (p. 14). Finish as you like.

18–15

18–17

18–19

18–18

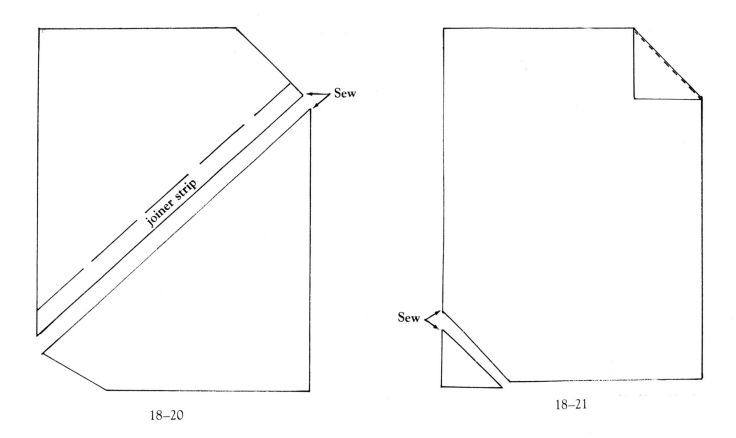

Sew

joiner strip

18–20

Sew

18–21

Field of Flowers (57 × 78 inches)

19 Field of Flowers

This very attractive little girl's quilt is relatively easy to make. The inspiration for this design can be found in some military banners dating from 600 A.D. However, the more rigid military look has been softened, and, with a little adjustment, flowers have emerged.

YARDAGE

Fabric A (background color)	3¾ yards
Fabric B (main color of flowers)	1¾ yards
Fabrics C to F (colors inside flowers)	¼ yard each
Second border	1 yard
Third border	1½ yards

CUTTING

Fabric A (cut six strips into forty-eight 4½ × 2½-inch rectangles)	twelve strips 2½ × 45 inches
Fabric A	twelve squares 12 × 12 inches
Fabric B	twelve strips 2½ × 45 inches
Fabrics C to F	three strips 2½ × 45 inches
Second border	eight strips 4 × 45 inches
Third border	eight strips 5 × 45 inches

SEWING DIRECTIONS

Place 1⅛ yards of fabrics A and B down, right sides together, on your work surface. (Read how to sew right triangles at the beginning of this book.) Graft the forty-eight squares on the back of fabric B, and sew as directed. When done sewing and cutting you should have a total of ninety-six triangle-squares. Press flat, and set them aside.

Place a fabric A strip faceup on your sewing machine. Lay a fabric B strip facedown on Fabric A strip with right sides together, and sew the length. Repeat this three times in all. Reread Strip Sewing in the Speed Techniques section of this book, p. 11.

19–1

Now let's build on this. Place your fabric combo faceup on your sewing machine with fabric A to the left, and place a fabric C strip facedown on Fabric B of the combo, with right sides together. Sew the length of the strips. Repeat until all three have had a fabric C strip added. (See 19–1.)

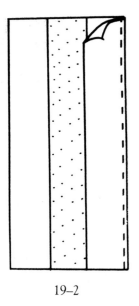

19–2

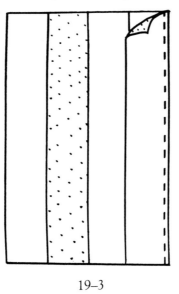

19–3

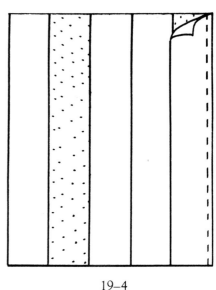

19–4

Place your fabric combo faceup on the machine with fabric A to the right. Place fabric D facedown on fabric C of the combo, right sides together. Sew the length of the strips. Repeat until you have added fabric D to all three. (See 19–2.)

Still building on the fabric combination, lay the fabric combo faceup on your sewing machine with your fabric A on the left. Place a fabric B strip on top of fabric D of the combo, right sides together. Sew the length of the strips. Repeat until all three fabric combos have a second fabric B added. (See 19–3.)

This will be the last strip added to this fabric combo. Place your fabric combo faceup on the machine, keeping fabric A to the left. Lay a fabric A strip facedown on fabric B of the combo, and sew the length of the strips. Repeat until all three fabric combos have a second fabric A added. (See 19–4.) Press your fabric combos flat, and set them on your cutting surface.

Lay your fabric combos, one on top of the other, making sure they lay smooth. (We will be cutting through all three layers at once.) Even off the top and measure down 2½ inches and cut. Do this all the way down. You should get about sixteen cuts from each strip. (See 19–5.) Place the pieces in a pile, and set them aside.

Now we are going to start our second combination, and we'll be working with this one for a while. Place a fabric E and a fabric B strip right sides together, and sew the length. Repeat this three times in all.

Lay your second fabric combo faceup on the sewing machine with fabric E to the left, and lay another fabric B on top of the other fabric B, right sides together. Sew the length. Repeat until all three combos have a second fabric B added. (See 19–6.)

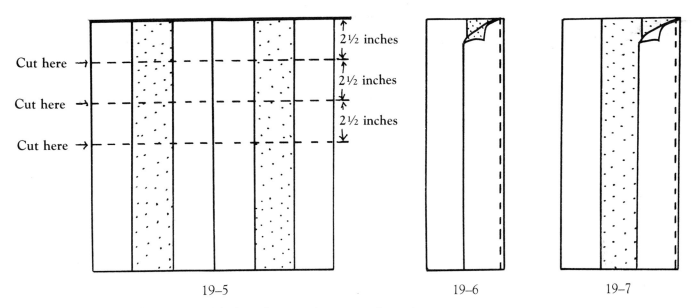

19–5   19–6   19–7

This will be the last strip added to this combination, but after it's cut we'll still be adding to it. So, don't get too excited.

Lay your fabric combo faceup on the machine with fabric E to the left. Place the fabric F strip facedown on fabric B, right sides together; sew the length of the strips. (See 19–7.) Press flat.

Lay your fabric combo one on top of the other, making sure they lay flat. Even off the top. Measure down 2½ inches, and cut. Do this all the way down. (See 19–8.) You'll get around sixteen cuts from each of the strips. Take twenty-four off the top, and set the rest of the combo pieces aside.

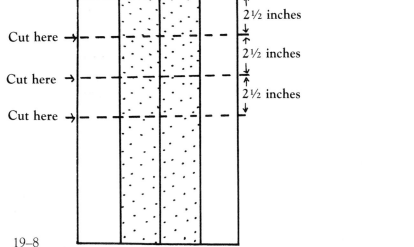

19–8

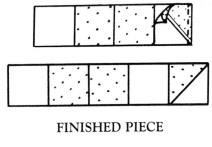

FINISHED PIECE

19–9

113

Lay one of your twenty-four strips of squares faceup on your sewing machine with the fabric E to the left. Working with the triangle-squares, place a triangle-square facedown on fabric F, right sides together, making sure that the fabric B triangle is in the upper right corner. (See 19–9.) Repeat until all twenty-four strips of squares have a triangle-square added. Now let's flip this strip over so that we can add a triangle-square to the other side.

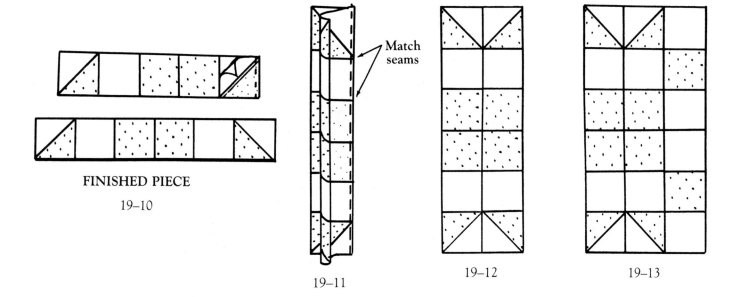

FINISHED PIECE

19–10

Match seams

19–11

19–12

19–13

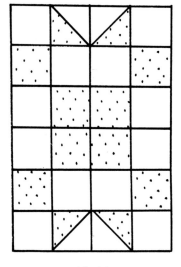

19–14

Place your strip of squares faceup on the machine with the triangle-square to the left. Lay a triangle-square facedown on fabric E with the fabric B triangle in the lower right corner. (See 19–10.) Sew and repeat until all twenty-four strips have a second triangle-square added. Press flat.

Still working with these strips of squares, lay a strip vertically on your machine as shown in 19–11. Lay another strip of squares facedown so that when it is sewn, it will look like 19–12 when opened up. This is the center of our flower. Repeat twelve times. Press flat.

Now we will work with the strip of squares from our first fabric combo, as well as the center of our flowers. Place the center of the flower vertically faceup on the sewing machine. Lay a strip of squares facedown, matching the seams, and sew so that when it is opened up, it will look like 19–13. Repeat twelve times.

Flip it over so that we can add a strip of squares to the opposite side. (See 19–14.)

Add a strip of squares to the opposite side of the flower's center as shown in 19–14. Press flat and set aside. This is the body of your flower.

Field of Flowers

We should have forty-eight triangle-squares left. Place two triangle-squares with right sides together. Sew them so they look like 19–15. Repeat twenty-four times.

Place your newly sewn triangle-squares faceup on the machine. Place one of the 2½-inch-by-4½-inch fabric A rectangles facedown, with right sides together, and sew as shown in 19–16. Repeat twenty-four times.

Flip the end of your flower over, and add a 4½-inch-by-2½-inch rectangle to the other side so that when finished it will look like 19–17. Repeat twenty-four times. Press flat.

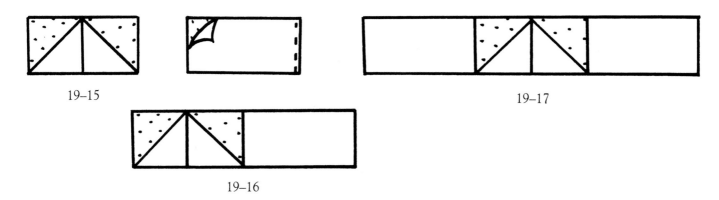

19–15

19–17

19–16

Place the body of your flower vertically faceup on the sewing machine. Lay an end piece facedown, right sides together, and sew so that when it is finished it will look like 19–18. Repeat this twelve times. Flip the flower over, and add an end piece to the opposite side so the finished block will look like 19–19.

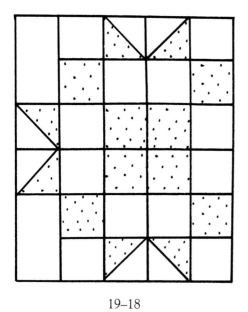

19–18

19–19 **FINISHED BLOCK**

116

Although it took many words to describe how to do this, it really wasn't very hard—was it?

You should now have twelve pieced blocks and twelve solid blocks. Your quilt top will have five rolls in it, with each roll having four blocks. Rolls 1, 3, and 5, start with a pieced block. Rolls 2 and 4 start with a solid block and alternate with a pieced block. This is the body of your quilt.

You thought I forgot all about those pieced strips you have from your fabric combos, didn't you? Well, I didn't. There are two things you can do with these:

A. Make more triangle-squares and construct more flower blocks for a sampler quilt or another Field of Flowers quilt.

B. This is the one I choose most of the time: If you look at the photo, you'll see a pieced border. I sew a strip from the first fabric combo to a strip from the second fabric combo, and then I keep alternating until I have two pieces long enough for the sides of the quilt. I follow the same step until I have two pieces long enough for the top and bottom. Then I attach them to the quilt body.

Following directions on attaching borders (p. 14), complete bordering your quilt, and finish it as you desire.

Fruit Dish (76 × 76 inches)

20 Fruit Dish

The Fruit Dish quilt looks difficult, but it is really quite easy to construct. The quilt is based on a checkerboard pattern that dates back to the 13th century.

YARDAGE

Light color (the fruit)	1¼ yards
Dark color (the fruit)	1¼ yards
Medium color (the dish)	½ yard
White	1¾ yards
First border	¾ yard
Second border	1 yard
Third border	1¾ yards

CUTTING

Light color	fifteen strips 2½ × 45 inches
Dark color	fifteen strips 2½ × 45 inches
Medium color (cut into twenty-five squares 5 × 5 inches; then cut on the diagonal into triangles)	four strips 5 × 45 inches
White (cut into fifty squares 4½ × 4½ inches)	seven strips 4½ × 45 inches
White (cut into thirty-eight squares 5 × 5 inches; then cut on the diagonal into triangles)	five strips 5 × 45 inches
First border (top and bottom)	four strips 2½ × 45 inches
First border (sides)	four strips 3 × 45 inches
Second border (top and bottom)	four strips 3 × 45 inches
Second border (sides)	four strips 4 × 45 inches
Third border (top and bottom)	four strips 4 × 45 inches
Third border (sides)	four strips 5 × 45 inches

When cutting be sure to first cut strips, then squares, and cut the squares on the diagonal to form triangles.

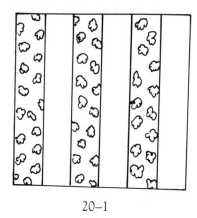

20-1

SEWING DIRECTIONS

Working with our light and dark 2½-inch strips, we will be making a checkerboard. This will be done by sewing light, dark, light, dark, light, dark, strips down the length. (See 20–1.)

Repeat twenty-five times. Press flat.

Measure down 2½ inches from the top, all the way across, and cut. (See 20–2.) Continue to measure 2½ inches down the length of the sewn sheet, and cut until you reach the bottom of the sheet. You will get fifteen to eighteen cuts for each sheet.

We will be sewing our strips of squares together to form a checkerboard. Each checkerboard will be made of six strips of squares sewn together. (See 20–3.) You will need thirteen checkerboards.

Press flat, cut on the diagonal (see 20–4), and set aside.

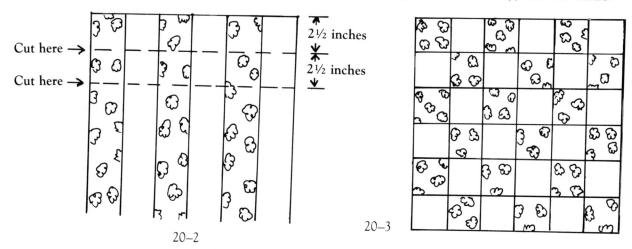

Cut here →
Cut here →
2½ inches
2½ inches

20-2

20-3

Now we will be sewing group A. Place a 4½-inch white square faceup on your machine. Lay a white triangle facedown so that the diagonal runs from the lower left corner to the upper right corner. (See 20–5.) Sew a total of twenty-five squares and triangles this way.

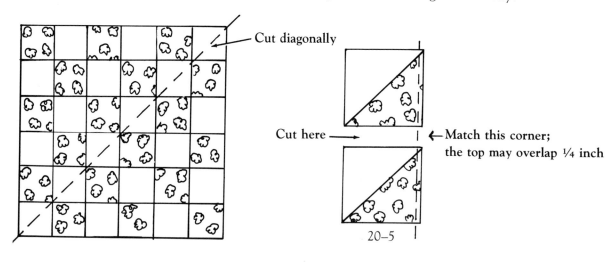

Cut diagonally

Cut here →

← Match this corner;
the top may overlap ¼ inch

20-4

20-5

120

Open up, and lay one of the twenty-five sewn white squares and triangles right side up on your sewing machine, so that the white triangle is to the left and the diagonal runs from the far left to the right. (See 20–6.) Lay a medium color triangle facedown so that the diagonal runs from the lower left corner to the upper right corner. (See 20–7.) Sew. Repeat for a total of twenty-five.

Now attach a white triangle to the diagonal of the colored triangle. (See 20–8.) Repeat twenty-five times in all. Press open and set aside.

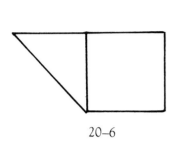

20–6

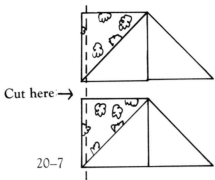

Cut here →

20–7

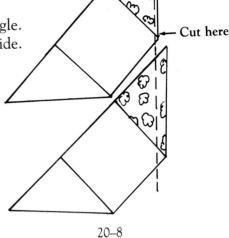

←— Cut here

20–8

Now we'll be working with group B. Place a 4½-inch white square faceup on your sewing machine. Lay a white triangle facedown, with the diagonal going from the upper left corner to the lower right corner (see 20–9), and sew.

Repeat twenty-five times in all. Open up and lay flat.

Lay the newly sewn group B faceup on your machine with the attached triangle towards the top and the diagonal running from the upper left corner to the lower right. (See 20–10.) Place a colored triangle facedown on the lower square with the diagonal running from the upper right to the lower left. (See 20–11.) Sew twenty-five in all.

Press flat. Now we will be working with both groups.

Lay one from group A faceup on your machine with the two sewn triangles toward the top. (See 20–12.) Lay one from Group B facedown with the square towards the top (see 20–13) and sew the length. Repeat twenty-five times in all. This is the completed fruit plate. Press flat.

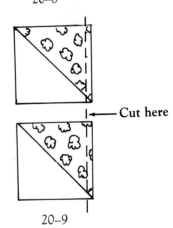

←— Cut here

20–9

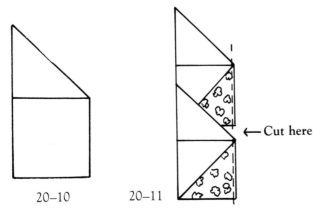

20–10   20–11   ← Cut here

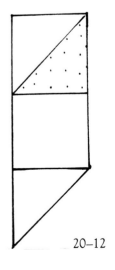

20–12

Fruit Dish

Lay your fruit plate faceup on your sewing machine. (See 20–14.) Lay your fruit facedown on the plate, making sure the seams of the plate match up with the center triangles of your fruit, and sew the length, taking care not to stretch your fabric. (See 20–15.) There will be some "give" in the fabric, since it has been cut on the bias. Repeat twenty-five times in all. Press the seams open.

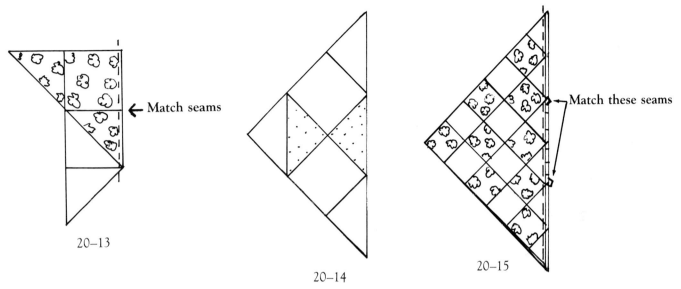

20–13

← Match seams

20–14

20–15

→ Match these seams

Sew with seams toward darkest color

Sew your blocks together to form the top. Your quilt will be five rolls deep.

five blocks = one roll

Once the body of the quilt is sewn together, it's time to add the borders. The borders were cut so that the widths for the top and bottom are slightly narrower than the sides. Refer to the section on borders (p. 14) to attach them to the body of your quilt. Make sure the thinner borders are on the top and bottom.

Finish the quilt as you like.

Helpful Hints

- Always prewash your fabrics.
- Fraying is usually a problem when prewashing fabric. To prevent this, snip off a corner at a 45-degree angle on both ends of the fabric, not each corner. Make the cut only about 1 to 1½ inches.
- Set your machine for 10 to 12 stitches per inch.
- When sewing, use a quarter-inch seam allowance.
- For a lovely finished quilt, take time to cut, sew, and press your pieces accurately.
- When joining two pieces that already have seams, sew seams in opposite directions to avoid bulk.
- When pressing seams, press them towards the darkest fabric to avoid a shadow behind light colors.
- Do you need a ruffle for a pillow and hate to gather? Zigzag over a piece of twine or crochet thread on the fabric you want ruffled, then pull the twine gently. It will gather neatly.
- Label quilts with your name and date. Here are some ways to do this: Use a permanent marker; cross-stitch the label on the quilt with waste canvas; or take a piece of white cotton fabric and type the information, then slip-stitch the label into place.
- To keep the knots in place when tying your quilt, apply a drop of waterproof glue.
- When hanging a quilt on a wall, rotate it every six months or so. First hang it from the top, then from the bottom, since the constant pull on the threads can cause them to break.
- Share quilting with a friend.
- Make a heavy-duty template out of a plastic lid from soft margarine. If it is slippery, rough up the back a little with sandpaper.
- I hate rethreading my sewing machine every time I run out of thread. So, I tie the end of the old thread to the end of the new thread. Then I continue to sew. As I'm sewing, the new thread will run through the machine, being pulled along by the old thread. When the knot arrives at the needle, I cut it off, thread my needle, and continue sewing.
- Never use nails or tacks to hang your quilts. Why put holes in your quilt? And eventually it will sag, making the holes even bigger.
- When storing your quilt, never keep it in plastic. Since plastic does not breathe, it allows moisture and insects to keep your quilt company until you air it out again.
- Air your quilt out and refold it in different directions every 3 or 4 months. Place it in a box lined with cotton sheets.

Quilting Terms

Backing	the bottom layer of your quilt
Bar Tack	zigzagging over a piece of yarn or ribbon, used in machine-tying a quilt
Batting	filling that goes between the quilt top and the backing
Bias	a true 45-degree angle on a woven fabric
Binding	a strip of fabric used to enclose the raw edge of all three quilt layers—top, batting, and backing
Chain Stitching	sewing pairs of pattern pieces one right behind the other without cutting the thread connecting them—done on a sewing machine
Finger Press	rubbing up and down with your finger and applying pressure at the same time to form a crease
Grain	the direction of the threads in your fabric—*lengthwise* grain runs parallel to the selvage edge; *crosswise* grain has more stretch than lengthwise grain and runs perpendicular to the selvage edge
Grid	evenly spaced horizontal and perpendicular lines
Loft	the thickness of the fiber; in quilting, the thickness of the batting
Patchwork Quilt or Patched Quilt	small pieces of fabric appliqued on a full-size piece of unbleached cotton
Pieced Quilt	small pieces of fabric sewn together to create a pattern
Pivot	a needle on which, in this case, fabric will turn
Quilt Top	the top layer of what will become your coverlet, or quilt
Sashes	pieces of fabric used to frame patchwork blocks
Selvage	the finished edges on both sides of a woven fabric
Template	a pattern shape used to trace or cut a design for a pieced or patchwork quilt

Tie Points	marks where the pieced top will be tied	
Tri-Squares or Triangle-Squares	the same as a half-square triangle	
Tying	a way of holding together three layers of the quilt	
Whipstitch	a small overcast stitch	

Metric Equivalents

INCHES TO MILLIMETRES AND CENTIMETRES

INCHES	MM	CM	INCHES	CM	INCHES	CM
⅛	3	0.3	9	22.9	30	76.2
¼	6	0.6	10	25.4	31	78.7
⅜	10	1.0	11	27.9	32	81.3
½	13	1.3	12	30.5	33	83.8
⅝	16	1.6	13	33.0	34	86.4
¾	19	1.9	14	35.6	35	88.9
⅞	22	2.2	15	38.1	36	91.4
1	25	2.5	16	40.6	37	94.0
1¼	32	3.2	17	43.2	38	96.5
1½	38	3.8	18	45.7	39	99.1
1¾	44	4.4	19	48.3	40	101.6
2	51	5.1	20	50.8	41	104.1
2½	64	6.4	21	53.3	42	106.7
3	76	7.6	22	55.9	43	109.2
3½	89	8.9	23	58.4	44	111.8
4	102	10.2	24	61.0	45	114.3
4½	114	11.4	25	63.5	46	116.8
5	127	12.7	26	66.0	47	119.4
6	152	15.2	27	68.6	48	121.9
7	178	17.8	28	71.1	49	124.5
8	203	20.3	29	73.7	50	127.0

YARDS TO METRES

YARDS	METRES	YARDS	METRES	YARDS	METRES	YARDS	METRES	YARDS	METRES
⅛	0.11	2⅛	1.94	4⅛	3.77	6⅛	5.60	8⅛	7.43
¼	0.23	2¼	2.06	4¼	3.89	6¼	5.72	8¼	7.54
⅜	0.34	2⅜	2.17	4⅜	4.00	6⅜	5.83	8⅜	7.66
½	0.46	2½	2.29	4½	4.11	6½	5.94	8½	7.77
⅝	0.57	2⅝	2.40	4⅝	4.23	6⅝	6.06	8⅝	7.89
¾	0.69	2¾	2.51	4¾	4.34	6¾	6.17	8¾	8.00
⅞	0.80	2⅞	2.63	4⅞	4.46	6⅞	6.29	8⅞	8.12
1	0.91	3	2.74	5	4.57	7	6.40	9	8.23
1⅛	1.03	3⅛	2.86	5⅛	4.69	7⅛	6.52	9⅛	8.34
1¼	1.14	3¼	2.97	5¼	4.80	7¼	6.63	9¼	8.46
1⅜	1.26	3⅜	3.09	5⅜	4.91	7⅜	6.74	9⅜	8.57
1½	1.37	3½	3.20	5½	5.03	7½	6.86	9½	8.69
1⅝	1.49	3⅝	3.31	5⅝	5.14	7⅝	6.97	9⅝	8.80
1¾	1.60	3¾	3.43	5¾	5.26	7¾	7.09	9¾	8.92
1⅞	1.71	3⅞	3.54	5⅞	5.37	7⅞	7.20	9⅞	9.03
2	1.83	4	3.66	6	5.49	8	7.32	10	9.14

Indian Homeland, see p. 84.

see p. 84.

Index